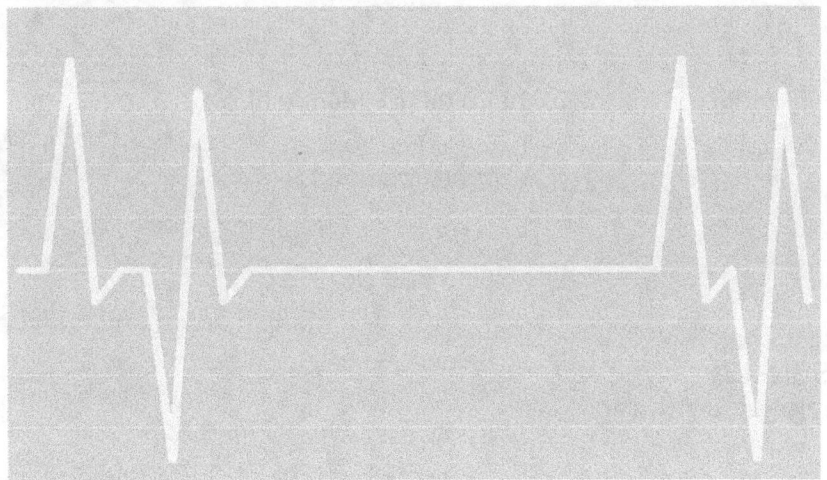

Down But Not Out

Hope and Help for the Unemployed

Luther M. Maddy III, Ph.D.

Down But Not Out:
Hope and Help for the Unemployed

© 2014 Luther M. Maddy III

All rights reserved.

ISBN-13:
978-1494746636

ISBN-10:
1494746638

Contents

Part I: Getting from Un- to Re- Employment

A note from the author 3
This is not how you planned it 5
It's all about attitude 13
It's time to act your age 29
It is time for an audit 39
The résumé: fact, fiction, or somewhere in between 49
When good interviews go bad 55
Preparing for your next interview 61
Back to school? 71
Working outside the box 85
What do you want to be when you grow up? 97
Some careers to consider 107
When the wolves are at the door 115
After you have the job… 133

Part II: It's my story and I'm sticking to it

Voluntary and involuntary changes 139
A new start and risky behavior 145
Interview Hell 151
Transitioning into a new career 159

This book is dedicated to my wife Tracy who provided strength and support during my own career crisis. She also encouraged me to further my education and pursue my dream career. This book would also not have been possible without the many students who attended my vocational school in the midst of their own career crises.

Full size forms referenced in this book and other resources are available at: www.LutherMaddy.com

Part I:
Getting from Un- to Re- employment

INTRODUCTION

A note from the author

Hope is like the sun, which, as we journey toward it, casts the shadow of our burden behind us.
Samuel Smiles

Although this introduction occurs at the beginning of the book, it was written last. It was not until this book was complete that I could adequately define and introduce it. And, though it may seem illogical, the best way for you to understand the true purpose and design of this book is for me to first explain what this book is not.

This book is not a step-by-step guide to ending your unemployment. While it includes some important résumé and interviewing tips, this book is not intended to replace other job hunting and resume creation guides. Books and training on interviewing techniques and résumé tips will still be an important part of your journey from unemployment to re-employment.

This book is not intended to replace a career or re-employment counselor. You will still need the assistance and guidance of a competent counselor to assist you in this journey. Your counselor can provide one-on-one interaction and guidance not available from any book. Your counselor can also provide important insight if a career change is in your future.

DOWN BUT NOT OUT

This book is not intended to supplant your attorney or financial counselor. While it does include some general financial and legal considerations and guidelines, these are included merely to help you navigate your way through this journey. Hopefully, you will need neither professional legal help nor financial counseling. But, should that be this case, the information in this book will help you better prepare for that time.

This book was specifically designed to give you hope and encouragement in the midst of your unemployment. Your current situation may appear dire, but it is only temporary. However, how quickly you make it through to the other side and in what condition depends largely on how you approach your unemployment. Your attitude, in the long run, makes all the difference.

It is my hope that you will be encouraged as you read Down But Not Out. I also hope you will find some of the insights I share in its pages very useful. I hope you learn more about yourself and some positive steps you can take to improve your attitude during this difficult time. I hope that you will see that no matter how bad things look right now, they can and will get better if you approach your situation correctly.

I once heard as pastor discussing the tragic loss of his young daughter. In the beginning, he was sure he could never endure the heartache, turmoil, and profound sense of loss. He explained that the best advice he ever heard was, "You will never get over this, but you will get through it".

From some people, losing a job can be as devastating as losing a close loved one. If you are in the midst of your own career crisis consider taking the advice that pastor to heart yourself. You will get through this difficult time and hopefully, my story and the information I share in Down But Not Out will help you get through it faster and in better condition.

Luther M. Maddy III

CHAPTER ONE

This is not how you planned it

When adversity strikes, that's when you have to be the most calm. Take a step back, stay strong, stay grounded and press on.

L.L. Cool J

Maybe the pink slip you received with your paycheck was a complete surprise. Or, perhaps you saw the signs all around in the economy, in your company, or in the news, but still you kept hoping you could avoid the inevitable. You may have worked for the same firm for many years and expected to do so until you retired. Perhaps you recently changed jobs and unfortunately hitched your wagon to a falling star. Perhaps you poured everything you had into your own business that ultimately failed. Regardless of how you got here, this is now your new reality. You have joined the ranks of the unemployed.

Maybe you have already spent many years in the workforce. You may have been unemployed before, perhaps when you were younger. But now, things are different. You have paid your dues. You are no longer wet behind the ears. Simply put, you are a little older than many of those you worked with and unemployed is not where you planned to find yourself at this time in your life. Especially not after investing so much time, energy, blood, sweat, and tears in your former place of employment. If that place of employment was your own business, its failure may have cost you much or even all of your accumulated wealth.

Or, perhaps you just recently embarked on your career journey. You had your ascension up the corporate ladder carefully mapped out. Your career progression plan did not include unemployment at this or any other time, but here you are.

To make matters worse, you have watched the news, read the paper, or heard people talk. You know, that things are tough out there. You have heard horror stories of a single job opening sometimes resulting in hundreds of applications.

If you have been unemployed for more than a week, you have surely heard stories from others who are or were in your situation. They have probably added to your apprehension, telling you how long they have been unemployed or how long it took to get a new job. You have also probably heard about many people who were unemployed who ended up settling for jobs paying less than they made in the past, sometimes a lot less.

Greeting customers at the local super discount store could work, but that does not sound very appealing. The burger flipping joints are always hiring, but that is a far cry from the management, clerical, training, construction, sales, or production job you had before. And, that does not even begin to take into account the incredible disparity between what those jobs pay and what you were being paid.

As you are mulling over your prospects, you begin to think about your finances. There is that little detail of making the house payment, car payment, student loan payment, life insurance payment, credit card payments, and or medical bill payments. You may be the primary income source for your family. Your weekly unemployment checks do not even come close to the amount you need to break even each month and your savings account is dwindling or maybe even gone.

THIS IS NOT HOW YOU PLANNED IT

You probably did not need the above reminder to help you realize that you are in a crisis: a career crisis. You already knew that. And, that is probably why you picked up this book.

Your current situation may seem to have placed an impassable chasm in your career path. But there is hope. This book was designed is to help you navigate your way through this career crisis and keep your sanity in the process. It is intended to guide you while you are unemployed and give you some tools and the confidence you need to once again join the ranks of the employed. In summary, this book was designed to give you hope by letting you know that things will get better. It was also written to provide you with some practical steps to navigate through your career crisis and become reemployed.

Career stages

It is not the purpose of this book to bore you with theories. That is why we have college textbooks. However, some pretty intelligent people have studied thousands of people and their respective careers: talk about boring. Still, one of the theories that resulted from all that research may help you better understand yourself and your feelings at this time.

According to one theory, people enter different phases of their careers based on their age and number of years in the workforce. Soon after starting in a career, individuals enter the progression stage. In this stage individuals grow in their careers and ascend the ranks. The progression stage may involve aggressive efforts to progress. The progression phase may include further education and maneuvering to climb the corporate ladder. People in this phase may also change jobs or employers to achieve a better position.

If you were in the progression stage of your career, unemployment can be a real blow to your ego. You worked incredibly hard to get where you were and now all of your efforts seem wasted. The idea of starting over with a new company, or perhaps even a new career has no appeal whatsoever. Yet, this is where you have found yourself. You have no job and your career plans have been shattered.

Perhaps you have been in the workforce for several years. If so, you may have been in the maintenance phase of your career. The maintenance phase usually begins as people reach their forties and they remain in this stage until they near retirement. This is the stage in a person's career that is usually marked with stability and consistency. People in this stage have usually completed their aggressive attempts to rise in their career through job changes, burning the midnight oil, or political maneuvering.

People in the maintenance stage are fairly content with their positions. They have begun to look ahead to, and hopefully begin planning for, retirement. They are not afraid to enhance their skills and grow in their career, but they do not vigorously pursue change. People in the maintenance stage are rather comfortable and expect things to remain as they are until they choose to leave their place of employment on their own terms, either through retirement or through taking another, less stressful position in the company or agency.

If you were in the maintenance stage of your own career, then you may feel like the very foundation of your life was violently shaken when you became unemployed. Your comfort level was completely shattered. Chaos and uncertainty have replaced security and stability. The status quo is no more. Your future is not looking as bright as it was before unemployment.

Regardless of the stage your career was in, you are probably very anxious now. As your length of unemployment grows, so does your fear and anxiety level. The thought of starting over with a new job or even a completely new career is very unnerving. Perhaps you are even finding it difficult to concentrate or make decisions. You may have found yourself becoming depressed, withdrawing from others. Maybe you have seen yourself losing your patience and becoming angry with those closest to you, when they did not deserve such a response.

THIS IS NOT HOW YOU PLANNED IT

Rest assured you are not losing it. Though it may not seem like it right now, everything you are going through is completely normal. You are not the first to experience this and you will certainly not be the last. You are not alone in this situation. However, simply realizing this does not solve your problems or get you back into the workforce. But, you should take comfort in knowing that the path you are now following has deep ruts created by the multitudes of unemployed individuals who have traveled this path before you. And, if you look around, you will soon be keenly aware there are numerous others journeying with you on this path at this very moment.

So, now that you know you are reacting normally and are not alone, continue reading. In the pages of this book you will find encouragement, worksheets, and some practical steps you can take to help you survive your time of unemployment and reach your goal of re-employment.

DOWN BUT NOT OUT

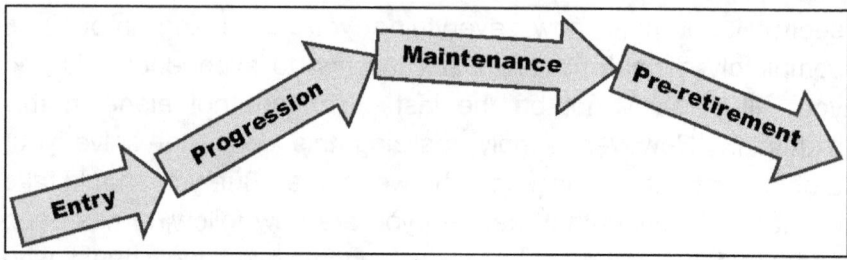

Figure 1: Normal Career Progression[1]

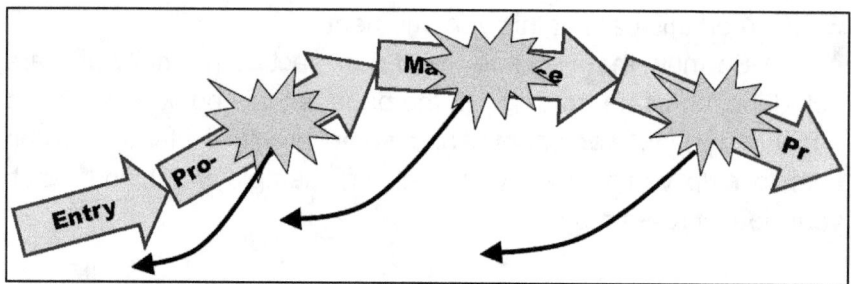

Figure 2: Career progression interrupted by unemployment

By trying we can easily endure adversity. Another man's, I mean.

Mark Twain

---

[1] Adapted from Donald Super's Career Development stages

THIS IS NOT HOW YOU PLANNED IT

Key Points/Action Steps

- Feeling like the foundations of your life have been shaken is completely normal.

- You are not alone. There are resources that can help
    - This book
    - Your local labor department
    - Support groups
    - Family, friends, and former co-workers

- Your natural career development cycle has been disrupted.

- Don't lose heart. You will get through this crisis.

CHAPTER TWO

It's all about attitude

How do you nurture a positive attitude when all the statistics say you're a dead man? You go to work.
                              Patrick Swayze

Your situation may appear dire right now, but it could certainly be worse. Sometimes that is difficult to realize when you are in the midst of the storm. However, no matter how bad things are for you right now, you probably do not have to look too far to find someone in a worse situation.

In the quote that opened this chapter, Mr. Swayze displayed a positive attitude in the midst of almost certain defeat. He knew his prognosis, but continued on with his life to the best of his ability. A positive attitude does not mean you ignore or deny your difficulties, but it does mean you do not wallow in them. Instead, a positive attitude means you face death, unemployment, bankruptcy, or any other difficult circumstances with dignity and with the realization that it could be worse. Yes, things could be worse, but they will almost certainly get better.

Along with the realization that your situation will eventually stabilize and likely improve, you must also realize that your attitude is an important key to surviving this ordeal. In many ways your attitude controls your current destiny. Maintaining a positive attitude will help you endure this temporary setback and will aid in your becoming employed once again. A negative attitude could keep you unemployed longer and cause your situation to become even worse.

Most people, even if they tell you otherwise, do not really want to hear your tale of woe. There are some exceptions to this that will be discussed later in this chapter. If you constantly dwell on your difficulties when you are with friends or acquaintances you will likely notice your circle of friends becoming smaller. People will start avoiding you. They will begin to think of you as someone who sucks the oxygen out of the room when you enter.

Your attitude will permeate all you do like family gatherings, church, the local bar, school, and even job interviews. If you are a miserable, unhappy creature that will come across loud and clear in any job interview. And, since nobody wants to work with unhappy miserable people by choice, they will likely offer the position to someone who appears to have a better attitude about life and work. The result of your negative attitude may be one more failed interview you can add to your list of rejections and failures. Now you have even more to be miserable about. Your negative attitude can create a self-fulfilling prophecy of doom.

Stop the cycle

You may feel that your current situation is out of your control. And, that may be the case for much of your situation. You certainly did not choose to become unemployed. You certainly did not choose to have difficulty finding a new job. You certainly did not choose your current financial difficulties and uncertainty. However, there is one aspect of your situation you can control: your attitude. How you choose to react to your circumstances is up to you. Leadership expert John Maxwell explains this fact by saying: "It is impossible for us to tailor-make

IT'S ALL ABOUT ATTITUDE

all situations to fit our lives perfectly. But it is possible to tailor make our attitudes to fit"[2].

A negative attitude is self-perpetuating and grows more negative with time. Unless you break the cycle of negativity, you will indeed become that unhappy, miserable creature. Instead, you need to break the cycle of negativity by learning to feel better about yourself and your abilities. And, while you may experience some apprehension about your future, you need to learn to embrace the change that your unemployment is bringing to your life.

As you examine the illustration below, notice that your attitude influences your actions. Your actions, in turn, influence or even create results. Continuing the cycle, your attitude is fed by the results you achieve. A positive attitude leads to positive actions and positive results. A negative attitude has the opposite effect.

So, how can you stop focusing on the negative? The answer is inside you. Or put another way, the answer is how you perceive yourself.

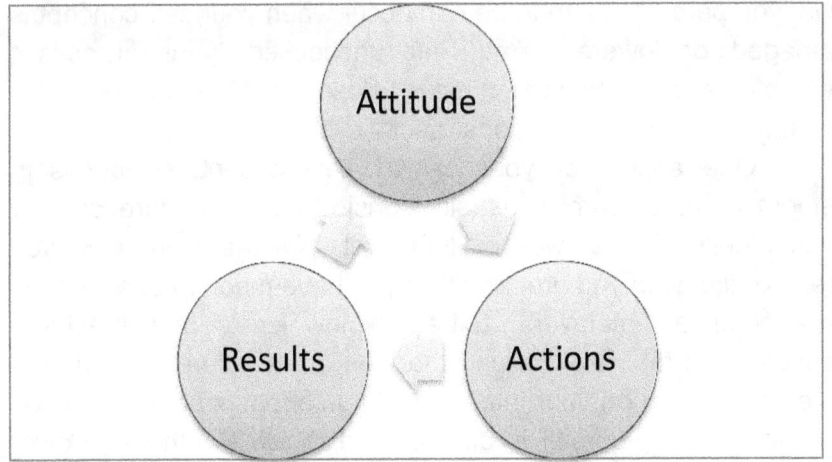

Figure 3: The attitude / actions / results cycle[3]

---

[2] Maxwell, John C. 1984. Your Attitude Key to Success

Your self-concept

An individual's self-image or concept is a fairly complex idea. A portion of your overall attitude, positive or negative, stems from the way you see yourself. Your attitude is often a reflection of your self-concept. Like career progression, the self-concept has been studied and studied again in an attempt to define it and see what affects it. Your self-image is essentially how you perceive yourself. It is not the self that others see, although that has some bearing on how you see yourself. Instead, it is the feeling and perceptions you have about yourself and your abilities at the deepest level.

Sometimes, such as during times of crisis, loss, or depression, a person's feelings about their worth and capabilities can become distorted in a negative direction. This distortion can cause a disparity between reality and an individual's perception. For example you may feel you have little worth and are not capable of learning new skills, doing well on a job interview, creating a résumé, or even performing the job you once did. However, in reality you are extremely knowledgeable and capable. The discrepancy between your true worth and capabilities, and what you perceive them to be can occur when your self-concept is damaged or lowered. And, left unchecked, your unrealistic perceptions can eventually move closer and closer to reality because of the attitude/actions/results cycle.

One aspect of your overall self-concept is your self-esteem. Self-esteem is usually considered a measure of your overall feelings of self-worth. High levels of self-esteem make you feel proud of who you are, and that you have much to offer society or a potential employer. Extremely low levels of self-esteem cause you to feel useless and that you are a failure. While self-esteem is based on your internal feelings about yourself, how you truly feel about yourself is difficult to disguise to others. Lower

---

[3] Adapted from Bandura, Albert. 1997. Self-efficacy: The exercise of control

self-esteem can be detected in your body language, attitude, and even in how you answer interview questions.

Another aspect of your self-concept is known as self-efficacy. Self-efficacy is a judgment of your capabilities to accomplish certain tasks. You probably had a considerable amount of self-efficacy at performing your last job. Like self-esteem, self-efficacy perceptions can differ from reality. You may feel you are not capable of doing well on a job interview when that is certainly not the case. Lowered levels of self-efficacy can hinder your job search activities. An individual with low self-efficacy may come across in a job interview as very unsure of his or her capabilities, when in reality he or she is perfectly capable of performing that job.

Many studies have found that unemployment often damages the unemployed individual's self-concept. Unemployment can result in lowered levels of both self-esteem and self-efficacy. The traumatic event of losing a job can cause some people to feel less capable then they actually are. Unemployment can be a blow to your self-esteem. It can cause you to begin to question your own self-worth.

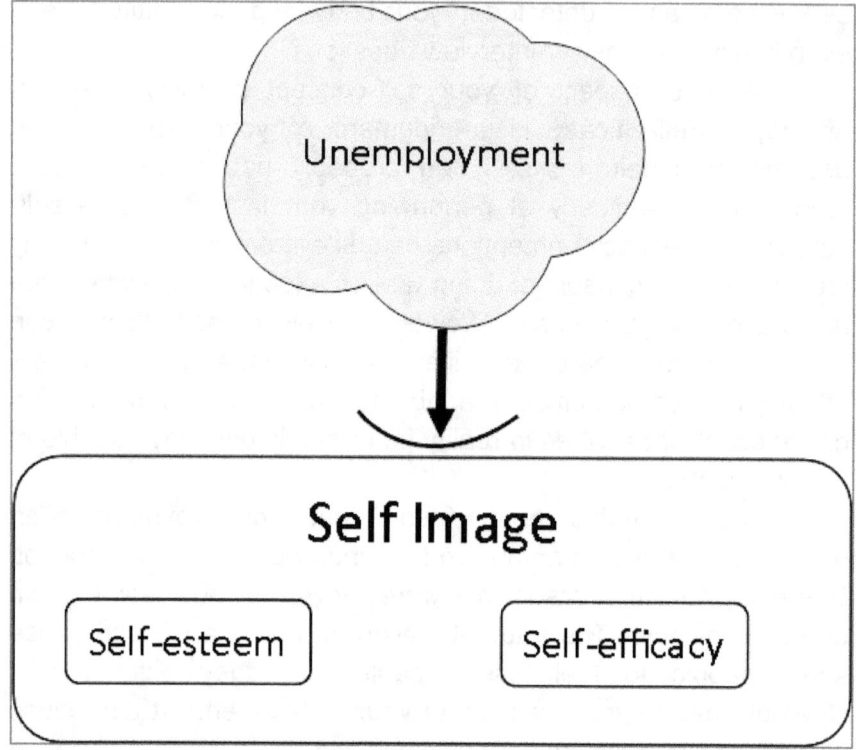
Figure 4: Unemployment can harm your self-image

    Perhaps you have noticed this in yourself since losing your job. You may have questioned whether you can even become re-employed. You may not even be sure you have what it takes to get another job or learn new tasks. If this is the case, realize these feeling are a natural result of your career crisis, but they are likely just perceptions, not reality.

    Good or bad, your age can also impact how unemployment affects your self-concept. If you are younger than 40 years of age, researchers have found unemployment can take a stronger toll on your self-concept than for those who are older. This may result from younger workers having fewer successes to look back on in their lives. With fewer experiences, younger workers tend to let their current situation contribute to feelings of lowered self-worth.

IT'S ALL ABOUT ATTITUDE

Older workers seem to negotiate the crisis of unemployment better than those a little younger when it comes to their self-image. With midlife comes the maturity to realize you are not defined by one single event in your life. You have many successes to look back on and that helps moderate the damage unemployment can do to your self-concept. People who have been in the workforce for many years have life experiences, good and bad to look back on. Living through other traumatic events lets experienced workers know they will likely also get through this event.

Regardless of your age, you probably understand your current unemployment does not define who you are. Nevertheless, a career crisis can certainly affect the way you feel about yourself at this very moment. And, being emotional creatures, sometimes it is difficult for individuals to think about past successes while in the middle of a crisis.

You will eventually get through this temporary setback. How quickly you reach the other side and in what condition depends more on you than you may realize. The key to surviving unemployment is your attitude.

Your self-concept affects your overall attitude. If you are feeling miserable, worthless, and incapable, this will translate into negative attitudes and feed the attitude/actions cycle. Instead, you need to take steps to improve your self-image and attitude right now. This will help you manage your mid-life career crisis and, most likely, get you re-employed faster.

So, how can you improve your self-image while you are unemployed?

1. Keep the Faith

Not everyone is spiritual or religious. However, for those who are, seeing your current condition as part of a larger plan may help you better accept your circumstances. Many studies of unemployed individuals have shown strong correlations between religious faith and higher values of self-concept. And, research has also shown that better self-concept tends to lead to shorter times of unemployment.

Seeing your unemployment as part of God's will or plan for your life helps begin answering those nagging questions like "Why is this happening to me?" In addition, spiritual faith can also provide reassurance that everything will be alright in the end, "all things work together for good…".

Those who profess a strong, intimate relationship with God also feel they can pour out their hearts in times of prayer. Prayer can be a time to express frustration, ask for guidance, or just a time of quiet mediation. Many studies have shown that prayer can aid healing and improve an individual's sense of well-being.

If you have a faith background with a personal God, this may be an excellent time to reconnect with that faith. Doing so may give you additional inner strength. And, depending of your faith background, the realization that God loves and cares for you as a person should give you a sense of worth and improve your self-esteem.

2. Find support

People need other people. People need people who will listen to them, support and encourage them, and even to call them out when they are wrong. Almost without exception, people need support from others. This is especially true for those who are unemployed.

Researchers have concluded that unemployed people with a strong social support network have a better self-concept than those who do not. In addition, research has also discovered a direct correlation between social support and engaging in activities that can lead to re-employment. In other words, those unemployed individuals who have someone to lean on during their difficulties are more likely to create résumés, apply for jobs, network with others to locate potential job openings, and participate in the job interview process. Strong social support directly contributes to shorter times of unemployment.

Unfortunately, there are times when those closest to you are not providing the social support you desperately need. Sometimes the individuals you look to for support may actually hinder rather than help your self-image. Researchers have found individuals in abusive or hurtful relationships suffer from lower self-image and usually do not feel confident in the job search process. If you find yourself in such a relationship, seek the help of a professional counselor and look for additional ways to get the vital social support you need during this time.

Your spouse or significant other is the most obvious and usually the most important supportive relationship during this time. However, when this relationship is not supportive or does not exist, you can also gain important support from close friends. You may even find social support by meeting with a group of acquaintances or others in a similar situation. Some places you can find social support include, but are certainly not limited to:

a. *Family and friends*

The first place to look for support during your time of unemployment is the social network you already have. Unless your family is very dysfunctional, many or most of its members will understand your need for encouragement and support. Talk to your family members. This is a perfect time to rekindle family relationships. Supportive family members will let you vent, but they may also offer advice. And, any advice they offer may certainly be worth listening to, even if you discount it later. Perhaps some of your family members have successfully negotiated their own career crisis.

If you are married or have a significant other in your life, let that person know that you are having a difficult time and need their support. Let that individual know that an encouraging home environment can help you get back to re-employment faster than a non-supportive or destructive home environment. Complaining and arguing about your situation with your spouse or significant other will likely contribute to the degradation of your self-image and your overall attitude. And that can eventually degrade your entire situation.

b. Job Clubs

Many churches, non-profit agencies, and even some state employment departments host or facilitate job clubs for the unemployed. The structure of these groups can vary from formal training sessions to simply sharing job leads and supporting one another. Formal group meetings may include résumé writing assistance and practice interviews. Even though you may not need training in the basics of the job search, the social support gained and the networking possibilities make these groups very worthwhile. Job clubs are also a great place to meet others who are either in your situation or have already come through to the other side.

There are two adages that can apply to job clubs, "strength in numbers" and "misery loves company". If you attend a job club or other support group that reminds you of the latter saying, find another one quickly. Many state labor departments maintain lists of job clubs meeting in their area. You can also do an internet search or contact your local church or other non-profit community support agency.

c. Professional counseling

If you feel you are dealing with more than you can handle or do not have a supportive family or social group, you should make arrangements to visit a professional counselor. Studies have shown that some people who become unemployed enter a grief cycle that is very similar to the grief level experienced when losing a spouse or other close loved one. People grieve differently, but if you find your current situation causing considerable turmoil in some or many aspects of your life, seek out a good counselor. Do not try to handle it alone.

There should be non-profit agencies in your area that provide free or inexpensive counseling. Your local labor department should be able to refer you to a counseling center. You can also try locating counseling through your local church or your local social services department. There is absolutely no shame in seeking help in dealing with your career crisis. Do not hesitate to use the tools available to you to get on the track to re-employment.

3. Stay active

One key to your attitude is staying active. Sitting at home all day waiting for the phone to ring or an email to suddenly appear in your inbox is not healthy. Numerous studies have shown strong correlations between activity levels and overall wellbeing and mental attitude.

Activity of any kind is useful, but activity that increases your appeal to potential employers is even better. Job clubs and support groups will get you out of the house and thinking about getting re-employed. In addition to these activities, consider volunteering at a church or other non-profit. You may be able to offer your expertise or manual labor to your local food bank, boys and girls club, or even a retirement community.

Ideally your volunteer activities should line up with your career goals. If you are considering a career change into the medical profession, consider joining the hospital auxiliary. If you are considering a teaching career, ask your local school district if there are any places you could volunteer your services.

Getting out of the house and into the workplace, even if only as a volunteer adds helpful structure to your life. It may also help provide a sense of meaning, something you may have lost upon becoming unemployed. And, if you target your volunteer activities correctly, you are making yourself known to potential employers. Impress them and your volunteer job may turn into a paycheck.

Adapt and survive

The work world today is quite different than that of just a few years ago. The only constant seems to be change. The demand for occupations shifts as do complete industries. Globalization, off shoring, and outsourcing will likely continue adding even more unpredictability to some career fields.

The industries, companies, and individuals that are able to adapt to these new realities will survive and even thrive. Rigidity, an unwillingness to change, is a route to almost certain failure during a career crisis. Those individuals who embrace change will not only find it easier to become re-employed, they will also come through the crisis with far fewer scars than those who insist on holding on to old skills, industries, and occupations.

Consider this quote from a book designed to guide career counselors to better help their clients during these constantly changing times:

> *We need to recognize that the most fundamental challenge that career counselors confront is to assist their clients to develop the skills of adaptation and resilience required to negotiate and use productively the fluctuating fortunes of their careers. It includes assisting clients to reinvent themselves continually, to identify opportunities, to recover from setbacks, to find meaningful work that matters to them and to others, and to capitalize on chance.*[4]

The key to sanity: an unbalanced life

If you envisioned a dream job at some point in your life but ended up somewhere else, this may be the perfect opportunity for you to do what you were always meant to do. You career is in a crisis at this point, you may as well make the best of it. Your goal should be to end up in a position that gives you more fulfillment and allows you to pursue a desirable balance in your life.

---

[4] Pryor, Robert & Bright, Jim. 2011. The Chaos Theory of Careers.

IT'S ALL ABOUT ATTITUDE

Think about your last job. Was it truly the job you envisioned? If so, then make every effort to reenter that career field. But even then, was that job supportive of a balance between family and work. Did your job sap so much of your time and energy that you had little left to give your spouse, other family members or friends? Did your last position contribute to you feeling you were making a difference in the world? Your current unemployment may be the perfect time to examine the career you had and the career you really want.

When you were working you strived to maintain balance in your life and probably experienced detrimental effects when you tended to over emphasize some areas of your life and neglected others. Though it may seem logical to spend most of your time and energy trying to become re-employed, this is not the best course of action. You need to strive to be well rounded, even while you are going through the turmoil of unemployment. Stay active, have some fun now and then. Get outside. Maintain relationships with friends and family.

Activities that keep you well rounded as an individual do not have to be expensive. You can take a stroll through a park, have a picnic, or invite some family or friends over for a potluck. While it may be your natural tendency to lock yourself in your house for the duration of your career crisis, this is not healthy and will likely prolong your period of unemployment.

The wheel chart in this section is an adaption of Paul J. Meyer's Wheel of Life. It illustrates the elements you should not neglect to maintain a balanced life. It has been modified to specifically fit the unemployed.

This representation of the Wheel of Life does not represent a life in perfect balance. Instead, it emphasizes a focus on friends and family, recreation, activity, exercise and spiritual growth. The larger sections of the wheel are the areas you should make a concerted effort to emphasize during your time of unemployment. Your natural tendencies will be to put most of your energies and efforts into finding a job, retraining for a new job, or trying to deal with your finances.

Conventional wisdom says once you are unemployed you should approach finding a new job as a full-time job. Yes, becoming re-employed takes work. However, you should not expend too much time or attention on the areas of your life you have little control over. Those areas include your employment status, your finances, and to some degree your education and training. Putting too much emphasis on these areas of your live may cause you to become too introspective and contribute to feelings of depression.

Instead, emphasize the areas of your life that will keep you whole and healthy. Emotionally healthy people are far more attractive to potential employers than those with an Eeyore syndrome. Eeyore was never happy and seemed to try his best to bring everyone else he encountered to his level of melancholy. No employer wants to hire an Eeyore if they can avoid it.

In addition to remaining healthy and whole there are other reasons to over emphasize some areas of your life. Support from friends and family is extremely important during your time of unemployment. Positive support will enhance your feelings of self-worth and improve your chances of getting hired. Use your time of unemployment to strengthen your relationships with family and friends. Recreate when you can. Keep active and exercise. Grow spiritually. Spending ample time in these areas of your life will give you the physical and emotional fortitude you need to apply for potential jobs and appear healthy at the interviews.

IT'S ALL ABOUT ATTITUDE

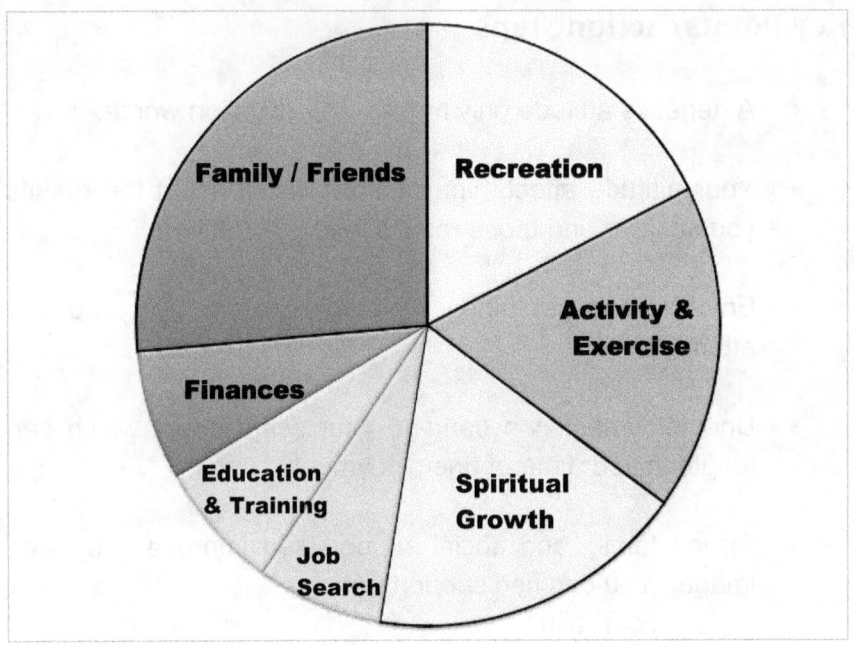

Figure 5: Life areas to emphasize during unemployment

"If you don't like something, change it. If you can't change it, change your attitude."

Maya Angelou

Key Points/Action Steps

- A negative attitude only makes your situation worse.

- Your attitude affects your actions which affect the results you achieve and those results feed your attitude

- Employers avoid hiring miserable people with negative attitudes.

- Unemployment can damage your self-concept which can lengthen your time of unemployment.

- Strong family and social support can improve your self-image. You can find support from:
    - Your faith
    - Family and friends
    - Job clubs and support groups
    - Professional counseling.

- Over emphasize some aspects of your life
    - Stay active. Don't sit home and wait for something to happen.
    - Strengthen relationships with friends and family

CHAPTER THREE

It's time to act your age

Aging is not lost youth but a new stage of opportunity and strength.

Betty Friedan

If you 40 or over....

Age and aging are relative. Regardless of your chronological age, the fact that you are reading this book is proof that you are not yet ready to leave the workforce. Perhaps you have twenty or more years of employment ahead before you reach the age at which you plan to retire. So, instead of thinking about your age as a detriment, it is time to begin thinking about how your age can benefit you and your new employer.

The Age Discrimination in Employment act became law in 1967. It was meant to protect older workers. This act prohibits employers from failing to hire someone based solely on age. This act also eliminated the practice of mandatory retirement for many jobs. This act created a protected class of individuals and, if you are over 40, you are in that protected class.

Well, since age discrimination is illegal, you can relax. You do not ever have to worry about an employer hiring someone younger than you, when you are both qualified for the position. Right. And Santa Claus really rides around in a sleigh powered by flying reindeer. Or, maybe it was flying pigs.

Simply making something illegal does not eliminate the practice. Speeding is against the law. So is talking on a cell phone or texting while driving in most states. Laws do not prevent illegal actions. Instead, they simply establish penalties for the behavior that serve as a deterrent.

Age discrimination happens. It happens often, but is difficult to prove. Who do you think the young, single male executive will hire to work in his office? You, or the proactively dressed young woman with similar or even inferior skills.

Maybe something like this has happened to you. You could try suing for age discrimination, but the executive will likely be able to prove the younger person can type a little faster, has better computer skills, or understands social media better than you do. As Bill Handel likes to say on his radio show, "you have absolutely no case." Age discrimination happens. Now get over it. And think about it, do you really want to work for an employer that values appearance or youth over competence?

Instead of focusing on the negatives of your age, it is time to focus on the positives. Seeing your age as a potential detriment will adversely affect your overall attitude. Age, and the wealth of skill and experience that come with it, can substantially benefit any employer. Here are just a few of the positive aspects of growing older you can emphasize to a potential employer.

Older and wiser

There is a considerable amount of truth in the adage that wisdom comes with age. Think about your own life. As you have grown older, hopefully you have learned to make better decisions than when you were younger. You have years of decision making experience and perhaps you have even experienced some consequences of bad decisions you made in the past. Both the good and bad decisions you have made in the past and the consequences of those decisions help guide your decision making process today.

IT'S TIME TO ACT YOUR AGE

Older and wiser does not mean getting stuck in the "we've always done it that way" routine. But, older and wiser does mean you probably have better decision making abilities than younger applicants. While you should not be afraid to try new ideas, you have the wisdom to think things through based on your previous life experiences.

What this means to a potential employer is that you can be counted on to consider both the pros and cons of any important decision. Rather than rushing to judgment before having all the facts or being a "yes" person for the boss, you will take your time and use all your analytical skills before making a decision.

A little slower now

At first glance, this may not seem like a benefit at all, but it actually is. Rather than thinking of yourself as "slower" than younger applicants, think of being "less impetuous". You are not the hot headed, rash individual you were a few years ago. You do not fly off the handle nearly as much. Neither do you rush into making a decision without thinking it through.

Part of becoming older and wiser is taking time to evaluate options. You are probably much more conservative with your own finances now than in younger years. That conservatism and ability to evaluate options before reacting out of pure emotion is a significant benefit you can offer an employer.

Patience is another benefit of age. You probably do not become angry as easily as you did in your younger years. You have the patience to hear someone out instead of rushing to judgment. Being slower can be a very good thing for responsible employees.

With age also comes a little more aversion to risk. Think of it as caution rather than fear. The caution that comes with age can be a great moderator in a room filled with young risk takers, ready to gamble away the entire company.

Every company needs analytical, deliberating decision makers. And, if you are older, wiser, and a little more cautious, you are the perfect person for the job.

Stability

Becoming unemployed has probably shaken the foundations of your life, but even so, you are considerably more stable than when you were younger. There is likely less drama in your personal life than in your younger years.

Even if you do have a significant amount of drama in your life, because you are older, wiser, and a little slower, even that will not affect your ability to be a great employee. You have learned to separate home and work far better than many younger applicants.

You are also not as likely to be burdened with child care and child illness issues as younger workers. Employers are not legally allowed to ask questions about your family or marital status. While many interviewing coaches urge people to never volunteer this information, you may consider doing so if, and only if, that information positively illustrates your stability, commitment, and freedom from some of the issues that plague younger workers.

Even still, be very careful what you volunteer. For example, you may mention you have no children at home, but then mention you have grandchildren living with you or that you are the primary care giver of your elderly parents. A quick slip of the tongue and volunteering too much information may end up costing you a job. Volunteer cautiously if at all.

Stress your stability on your résumé and in interviews. Stability is another benefit of age that can be seen as a plus to almost every employer.

Attention span and work ethic

Some younger workers have the attention span of a gnat. Give them a computer to work with and they seem to spend most of their time on some social networking site telling the world what they are doing at work. Or, when they should be paying attention during the staff meeting, they are using their smart phone to tell the world what they are doing at that very moment.

IT'S TIME TO ACT YOUR AGE

You are older and wiser. You know that your time at work is for working. You pay attention to what is going on around you rather than worrying more about the world outside during work hours. You also are not afraid of hard work. You have done it for years and you know what it takes and you are willing to do just that.

Older workers rock!

You may recall that unemployment can damage your self-image. These last few pages were intended to give your self-image a boost, and perhaps a chuckle or two. Becoming re-employed often means selling yourself to a potential employer. To do that, you need to look at your age as a benefit rather than detriment. As you see your age and experience in that light, you will have a much easier time convincing a potential employer of the same thing.

Do not live in the past

One trap people fall into as they age is spending more time looking back than forward. You have many accomplishments in your career. And, yes a potential employer may want to hear about a few of these. However, a potential employer is much more concerned with what you will do, not what you have done.

A potential employer is often interested in your total package. The total package includes your skills, attitude, personality, and appearance. This means to become re-employed you may have to make some changes. In the next chapter you will take an honest assessment of your skills, but for now think about your personality and appearance.

Take a few minutes and think about the impression your appearance gives, especially during an interview. Do not show up to an interview in the blue polyester leisure suit you found hanging in the back of your closet. Instead stay up to date. Your interview attire should match the organization and should be at least one level above the position you are applying for. Learn what is currently considered stylish in the business world and dress for that. Every detail of your wardrobe matters, even your shoes. New or nicely polished current shoes can make a difference.

How about your hair? Have you worn the same hair style since the 1980's? Or does your hair style portray you as older than you are or feel? Maybe now is the time to change your hair and even your wardrobe. If you cannot afford new clothing there are many resources available and some of these will be covered in a later chapter.

When you get to an interview you do want to emphasize your assets and age is actually one of those assets. However, you need to still be current. This means having current skills, but also being aware of current trends in that industry. It also means being aware of the current world around you.

You will often be interviewing with those who are younger than you. If this is the case, references about the Kennedy assassination, the Vietnam War, cassette tapes, payphones, and even William Jefferson Clinton, may fall on deaf ears and elicit confused looks. Instead, immerse yourself in the current happenings of the world. Be ready to discuss a variety of current events and culture at a cursory level. This includes topics like politics, sports, music, and most importantly, reality show stars. You want to be, and portray yourself as a well-rounded, up-to-date, interesting individual that would be a great asset to any workplace.

IT'S TIME TO ACT YOUR AGE

If you are under 40....

The key to re-employment is emphasizing your strengths, even when those strengths could be perceived as detriments. Age, for both younger and older unemployed individuals can be either one. Whether your age is perceived by a potential employer will depend largely on that employer and your ability to stress the benefits of your age.

Because age discrimination is illegal, you want to be careful how you emphasize your age. You do not want to make insulting statements about mature workers during a job interview. Aside from encouraging a potential employer to break the law you may be insulting some members of the interview panel. Instead, you simply want to discretely emphasize the benefits your youth can offer. Here are some things you might consider emphasizing to a potential employer.

Time left in the workforce

Remember the career stage theory? At your age you have years left to remain in the progression stage. You can invest years in a new employer and can grow with your employer. Stress that you see this new position as a career and intend to move up in the company, even though this may take some time. You have the time needed to do this. You will become an even more valuable employee as the years go by.

Technological savvy

You grew up with computers, smart phones and the Internet. Even if you do not have expertise in some area of technology, picking it up is easy for you. You do not require the level of training that workers who did not grow up with computers require. You are probably very comfortable with the latest method of social networking and other electronic communication. These are benefits you can stress on your résumé and during the interview.

Ability to multitask

While some people may call this a short attention span, you probably have the ability to talk on your cell phone, text, and check your social media page, while you are carrying on a conversation with someone in person. You do have the ability to quickly jump from one project to another, but even so, you are able to complete everything you need to do. Effective multitasking is a much needed skill in today's workforce. If this is one of your strengths, ensure you highlight that on your résumé or in the interview. However, remember that at work, multitasking means only tasks related to the job, not personal social networking, while you are on the clock.

A needed skill...

If you are fairly young, your preferred method of communication may be nonverbal. You may prefer tweeting, texting, or posting to talking on the phone or even in person. While there are some jobs that will allow you to communicate this way, verbal communication is still a very important skill in almost every occupation. In many occupations, verbal is the preferred or most important method of communication. If your verbal communication skills are lacking, this will become very apparent during an interview, over the telephone or in person. If your verbal communication skills need improvement, consider taking a class, or at the very least participating in some mock interviews at a support group, training center, or labor department.

Dress for success

Some items of dress and personal adornment are appropriate at some places of employment and not others. Research these policies before you show up for an interview. For example, some employers still have policies about visible tattoos. Others have policies about visible body piercings.

If a potential employer has policies concerning tattoos, piercings, or other even dress you should know that before the interview. You do not want to arrive at the interview wearing

IT'S TIME TO ACT YOUR AGE

shorts and Birkenstocks and find out the entire interview panel is wearing ties. It is a good rule of thumb to dress one level above the dress standard for the organization or company. So, if dress code business causal, then you should plan on dressing slightly above that standard.

Some jobs require that you deal with customers or coworkers in person. For these jobs consider covering any tattoos you can and removing visible piercings for the interview. After you are hired, you can relax into the standards of that organization or business.

The years teach much which the days never knew.

Ralph Waldo Emerson

Key Points/Action Steps

Mature workers:
- Mature workers have several advantages over younger workers including:
    - Decision making skills
    - Patience
    - Stability
    - Work Ethic

- Don't live in the past. Stress what you can do, not have done to potential employers.

- Stay current: Update your appearance, stay abreast of current culture and trends.

Younger workers:
- Stress your willingness to stay with the firm for the long haul

- Emphasize your technical savvy

- Practice verbal communication

- Consider what your appearance says about you

CHAPTER FOUR

It is time for an audit

Mastery is great, but even that is not enough. You have to be able to change course without a bead of sweat, or remorse.

Tom Peters

To get hired you need skills. Not just any skills, you need the specific skills the employer is looking for. Since you have already been employed, you undoubtedly have many useful skills. But, as you begin the process of becoming employed again, you will need to complete an honest assessment of your skills. Are your skills still relevant? Do your skills need some updating? It is time to add some new skills?

This section will help you evaluate your current skill set. As you complete a skills audit using the forms in this chapter, you will, hopefully, become more aware of your strengths and of some areas you need to improve. You may also find that some of your skills need refreshing or are completely obsolete. And, unfortunately, obsolete skills will not help you become re-employed.

Hard Skills

Hard skills can usually be measured or quantified. Gaining hard skills usually requires training or formal education. Hard skills do not naturally occur as a result of your personality, although your personality may lend itself to a specific set of hard skills. Operating production machinery, mechanical engineering, typing, using a spreadsheet, drawing blood, or operating heavy equipment are all hard skills. Hard skills may even come with licenses or certifications, such as a CPA or registered nursing.

Possessing a specific set of hard skills makes you qualified for certain jobs. When human resource professionals begin to look at résumés or applications submitted for an open position, the first thing they look for is a hard skills match. Applicants that do not possess the minimum hard skills required for the job will not usually make it past the first round. This illustrates why it is important to cater your résumé to the specific job for which you applying. This and other résumé tips will be covered in more detail in another chapter.

The life expectancy of some hard skills is very short, while others have a long life. For example, driving a semi-truck is a hard skill that has a fairly long life. Accounting is another example of a hard skill with a long life, but one that requires occasional enhancing as rules and regulations change. Other hard skills have a very short life and require regular refreshing or retraining. Web site and mobile application development would be examples of hard skills requiring constant retraining as new standards and programming languages evolve.

As you create an inventory of your hard skills, realize that some of those hard skills are obsolete and should be given the burial they deserve. Repairing cassette tapes may be a great skill, but you can no longer count on that to secure employment. Other obsolete hard skills may be salvageable if they are refreshed, such as in renewing an expired license or certification.

As you complete this audit, realize some obsolete hard skills may serve as an excellent foundation for learning newer

IT IS TIME FOR AN AUDIT

skills. For example, if the last word processing software you used was WordPefect 5.1 it is unlikely you will find that listed as a required hard skill for many positions today. But, the concepts of using a word processor remain essentially the same and having that knowledge will likely make learning the latest and greatest word processor easier for you than for someone starting from scratch.

To use the "Hard Skills" audit form, list all the hard skills you possess. Then, as you list each one, honestly assess that skill's viability in today's job market. You may wish to search your local newspaper job advertisements, job websites like CareerBuilder.com, or job listings maintained by your labor department to see if your skills are currently in demand. Spend some time in research to determine what employers are looking for in potential employees.

In doing this assessment you may find that some of the skills you held most dearly are obsolete. You may also be pleasantly surprised to find you do have skills that are currently marketable. Or, perhaps you have skills that could be very marketable with just a little bit of refresher training.

Professional Skills Audit				
Hard Skills (welding, computer applications, medical coding, bookkeeping, heavy equipment, etc...)	Current	Obsolete	In demand if current	Needs Refreshing

Soft Skills

Interpersonal and emotional skills fall into the realm of soft skills. Some soft skills are thought to be part of an individual's emotional intelligence quotient (EQ). Certain soft skills are also considered to be related to your personality. And, while you can receive training to better perform certain soft skills, some personality types generally have a propensity for certain sets of soft skills.

Some jobs rely more heavily on soft skills than others. The need for specific soft skills also varies from job to job. For example, a call center customer service representative will need different soft skills than a bookkeeper. Nevertheless, soft skills are an essential component of every job.

As mentioned previously, the hiring process for many positions begins with a screening based primarily on hard skills. The top few candidates are then interviewed in person or over the phone. The interview process is largely about determining how a potential employee would "fit" within the organization. The interview is, in large part, an assessment of your soft skills.

IT IS TIME FOR AN AUDIT

Mastery of essential soft skills can set you apart and bring you closer to the top of the list of the large pool of applications for the position.

As you make an audit of your soft skills, think about the positions you have previously held and the soft skills that were required, even if those skills did not appear in your job description. To help you analyze your soft skills, here are some to consider:

1. Communication: This is the ability to communicate your thoughts clearly to your coworkers, supervisor, or customers. All jobs require some form of communication, but some jobs require this skill to be especially refined. Communication involves both written and oral communication skills. If you have written instructions, procedures, company brochures, or other documents, you may have developed strong written communication skills. If you are an excellent speaker or are able to communicate instructions to your coworkers then you have developed your oral communication skills. If you are particularly gifted in one or the other, you may want to include it separately on your résumé where you can. For example, "excellent written communication skills" may appear on your résumé highlighting that aspect of communication.

2. Customer Service: This is a fairly generic term in itself and will not mean much if you list it just that way on your résumé. However, perhaps you have a skill for achieving customer satisfaction, even in situations where you begin with unhappy customers. Perhaps you work hard trying to make your customers happy and have received positive feedback about this from customers or your supervisors. As you are evaluating your customer service skills, remember that although you may not have dealt with external customers, every position has internal customers. Internal customers include those you work with and for.

DOWN BUT NOT OUT

Perhaps your positive attitude and work ethic cause you to excel at internal customer service. If you have a knack for making either internal or external customers happy, then you possess strong customer service skills.

3. Teamwork: Teamwork is essential in today's work world. Successful team management or membership is an important item for your soft skills inventory. Successful team players are listeners and willing to sacrifice independence and their own opinions to achieve team success. Excellent team members are open minded, but will also tactfully give feedback to other team members, even when that feedback is negative. Many businesses today use virtual teams. With today's technology, group collaboration is easier than ever before, even when other members of the team are separated by several time zones.

4. Sales: Sales differs from customer service in that it involves convincing customers they need something you can provide. Perhaps even something the customer did not know they needed until you enlightened them. Successful sales people are able to find a customer's need and then offer a solution to that need. Selling is indeed a skill and if this skill is in your strong set, you know it and enjoy sales.

5. Problem solving/critical thinking: If you think "outside the box" and can find solutions others cannot, you are strong in this skill. Critical thinking and problem solving involve looking at issues and problems from many angles and analyzing possible solutions before determining a course of action. Being able to think abstractly and not being afraid to experiment are also indicators you have strong problem solving skills.

IT IS TIME FOR AN AUDIT

6. Leadership: Leadership involves inspiring and motivating others to achieve a goal. Leaders clearly communicate vision and get others to "buy in" to it. Leaders inspire and instigate change. In short, leaders blaze the trail. If you have a talent for inspiring and motivating others toward a goal, then you should include leadership as one of your skills.

7. Management: This is the skill of creating and organizing systems and teams. Management skills are necessary to keep things working within the organization. Managers ensure people in their employ perform adequately and provide direction when needed. While leaders blaze the trail, managers pave it and install traffic lights. Managers are great at installing and monitoring systems to ensure everything works as it should.

8. Negotiating: Negotiators resolve disputes and bring about agreements. This requires the ability to clearly see both sides of an issue and strive for a "win / win" for both parties. Negotiators can listen both to what is being said and what is not being said to find terms that will satisfy both parties.

9. Training: Training involves the ability to instruct. This may include instructing a group or conducting one-on-one training. Training requires patience, organization, and subject knowledge. If you have this skill, ensure to include this on your résumé.

10. Time Management: Time management is the ability to manage your time to accomplish goals and tasks. Effective time management involves effectively setting priorities and ordering your time to complete those tasks

with the highest priority most in line with meeting your goals.

11. **Mentoring/Coaching:** Mentoring and coaching involves coming along side an individual to help them succeed. In the workplace, mentoring may include providing informal assistance to help an individual learn new tasks, or it could include formal meetings to review career progression and provide encouragement.

Use the "Soft Skills" form to honestly assess your soft skills. For each skill listed, place a mark in the appropriate rating column. There are also some blank lines for you to evaluate soft skills not listed on the form. After conducting a skills audit, you may realize your skill set is somewhat lacking. If this is the case, consider some training options. These options may include simple skill enhancement training or you may consider retraining for an entirely new career. Retraining options will be discussed in detail in a later chapter.

Professional Skills Audit				
Soft Skills	Absent	Needs Improvement	Satisfactory	Superior
Communication				
Customer Service				
Teamwork				
Sales				
Problem Solving/Critical thinking				
Management				
Leadership				
Negotiating				
Training				
Time Management				

IT IS TIME FOR AN AUDIT

A winner is someone who recognizes his God-given talents, works his tail off to develop them into skills, and uses these skills to accomplish his goals.
Larry Bird

Key Points/Action Steps

- Hard skills can become obsolete or outdated

- Soft skills are often personality based, but can be learned and improved upon.

- Retraining can help make your skillset more marketable.

CHAPTER FIVE

The résumé: fact, fiction, or somewhere in between

When you are asked if you can do a job, tell 'em, 'Certainly I can!' Then get busy and find out how to do it.

Theodore Roosevelt

Despite the obvious temptation, your résumé should never include falsehoods. The information age is alive and well and facts are easily checked. Non-existent degrees or places of employment may be easily discovered during the background check process. And, you really do not want to get a job under false pretenses only to find out later you are in over your head.

The "I can" attitude expressed in the quote from Teddy Roosevelt is far different than an "I can say I did that" attitude. The "I can say I did that" attitude usually results in modifying a résumé with inaccurate embellishments or misstatements to fit the advertised position. In contrast, the "I can" attitude displays a willingness to learn new tasks and shows you are not afraid of challenges. This is a great attitude to show a potential employer.

Type of résumés

After you have done an honest assessment of your skills, this next thing to do is put together a detailed list of your work experience. Then, you will merge the two to create the perfect résumé. Keep in mind that your résumé should not be a static document. While you might maintain one master template, your résumé should be created specifically for the job you are trying to get. Your résumé should highlight the skills the employer is hoping to find. Use the same skill terminology you see in the job listing. Match the job listing's wording and key phrases where you can do so honestly. The first selection round for many positions is little more than an electronic scan of résumés looking for key phrases and buzzwords, especially those listed in the job description or announcement.

After inventorying your skills and tracking down your work history, you then have to decide what résumé you want to create. Résumés generally fall into three categories chronological, functional, or combined. The category you choose will depend on your particular job history and the position you are hoping to secure.

The chronological résumé does what its name implies. This type of résumé displays your work history and experience in chronological order. A chronological résumé lists employers, job titles, and dates of employment. Chronological résumés make it very easy for a potential employer to see your career progression. The neat, orderly layout of this résumé format makes it the most common and readily accepted in the business world.

The chronological résumé is perfect if you have a work history that displays progressing responsibilities and career improvement. It is also perfect if your career history has no gaps. For example, if you dropped out of the workforce for a few years to raise children, try your hand at multi-level marketing, pay your debt to society, or even perform charity work abroad, the omission of a time period on your chronological résumé will likely cause you to be eliminated from consideration quickly.

THE RESUME: FACT OR FICTION

If you do have employment gaps, and choose to use the chronological résumé format, explain the gaps when you can. Fill in the missing time periods by explaining where you were attending school, or trying your hand at your own business during those time periods. If you have employment gaps that you do not want to or cannot explain, then the chronological résumé is not the best fit for you.

If you have employment gaps, do not despair. There is still a résumé format you can use successfully in your job search. That résumé format is the functional résumé. The functional résumé format deemphasizes the chronological listing of your work history and instead emphasizes your skills and abilities. The functional résumé is also a great format for younger workers with less work experience because it emphasizes skills rather than work history.

In a functional résumé, you place your skills and abilities at the top of the résumé. You still include your work history on a functional résumé but that usually appears at the bottom and is very general. If you properly emphasize your skills and abilities, a potential employer may be far more impressed with those than unimpressed by an employment gap. This will especially be the case if the skills you have listed are geared specifically to those listed in the job announcement.

There are some disadvantages of the functional résumé. First, some employers may not be familiar with this format and some simply dislike it. When a potential employer sees a functional résumé he or she usually recognizes that you are trying to hide a gap in your employment history. Realizing this, it is extremely important to list your skills as they relate to the specific job. This is still another argument for customizing your résumé for every submission.

A third résumé format is the combination format. The combination résumé includes a short summary of relevant skills and experience at the very top. Below that, it is laid out very similar to the chronological résumé. This format is excellent when you include skills and experience at the beginning of the résumé that match the job description or requirements, especially when you follow that up with a detailed and impressive chronological job history.

There are many resources available to help you create a perfect résumé. Very likely your state department of labor has many examples for you to examine. These departments also often provide résumé creation training and assistance. You can also find help and suggestions from job clubs and other support groups.

The truth, the whole truth, and nothing but the truth?

If you are testifying under oath you are not supposed to leave out any details. That is the whole truth. Obviously, your résumé cannot tell the whole truth about your job history. Listing everything you have ever done would take reams of paper and no perspective employer would even attempt to read it in its entirety.

Since you cannot include everything, you need to be selective about what appears on your résumé. If you are applying for a job managing a small retail establishment listing that you are certified to operate high tech robotic production equipment will only confuse the reader of your résumé and waste valuable space. A customized résumé should include only information pertinent to the job for which you are applying.

And that finally brings up the issue of flaunting your age on your customized résumé. Experts differ on whether or not you should consciously try to hide your age on your résumé. Some résumé consultants are adamant that you should never list dates that are more than 10 years in the past. Other consultants claim it makes no difference at all how far back your résumé goes.

How much historical data you list on your résumé will depend on which set of experts you choose to believe. However, there are some other things to consider. First assume you have an unbroken record of employment. You began your work life by flipping burgers for several years after leaving high school.

THE RESUME: FACT OR FICTION

Perhaps you were even promoted to supervisor. Listing your burger flipping career on your résumé will certainly date you. And, unless it is pertinent to the position you are hoping to be offered, there is no need to include that on your résumé. When deciding how much history to include on your résumé, the best answer is to only go far enough back to include skills and experience pertinent to your current job aspirations.

If you are a younger worker, then listing all of your work experience becomes very beneficial. If you have burger flipping experience, and just a few years of additional work to report, certainly include the burger flipping experience. Younger workers want to do everything possible to promote an image of stability and dedication to work.

If you decide to leave some work history off your résumé, ensure you do not create any gaps in the process. Listing an unrelated job is better than creating the appearance of a gap in your employment. Leaving a potential employer to guess what you were doing during an employment gap is not a good thing. You do not want your potential employer to simply assume the worst about the time period missing on your résumé. You want your résumé to display a stable work history, so be sure you include enough history to accomplish that.

Hitting the target with your résumé

Your résumé should be the arrow that hits the center of the target, the job you are applying for. The format you choose for your résumé, one of those discussed in this book or some other format is not as important as having it address the specific position. A generic résumé is not nearly as effective as one that targets a specific position.

When creating your specific résumé, review the job description or announcement very carefully. Look for the required skills and ensure your résumé addresses those specific skills. In addition, look for buzzwords, acronyms or technical terms the potential employer uses. When possible, add the same jargon to the résumé you submit for that position.

DOWN BUT NOT OUT

You will not create just one résumé to use until you are hired. Instead you should create different résumés for different positions. You do not have to start from scratch. Once you have your generic résumé, you can simply modify it to more closely fit a specific job. Résumés targeted to specific positions are considerably more effective.

> *If you call failures experiments, you can put them in your résumé and claim them as achievements.*
> Mason Cooley

Key Points/Action Steps

- Choose the résumé type that fits your situation

- Promote an image of stability and dedication to work.

- Explain obvious gaps when possible

- Do not make yourself appear older than you must

CHAPTER SIX

When good interviews go bad

I don't mind doing interviews. I don't mind answering thoughtful questions. But I'm not thrilled about answering questions like, 'If you were being mugged, and you had a lightsaber in one pocket and a whip in the other, which would you use?'

Harrison Ford

If it has not happened yet, rest assured it will: a good interview will go bad. Interviews can turn suddenly and without warning. For instance, you may be feeling quite confident about your interview up to the point one of the interviewers asks a question for which you were completely unprepared. Your stammering, unintelligible answer sets the tone for the remainder of the interview. Before long you are sweating, beginning to feel sick, and praying the interrogation will end soon.

While some interviewers may find enjoyment in bringing interviewees to the point of tears, they are certainly not the majority. Everyone in the interview process understands the interviewee is probably very nervous. Some stammering, pausing, and "I don't know" answers are expected and will not necessarily disqualify you from consideration. Instead, the purpose of the "lightsaber" question is to see how you handle stress or pressure, especially if those are part of the job you are interviewing for.

During the interview, do not be afraid to acknowledge you do not know something. It is far better to explain that you do not have the answer right now, but are very willing to learn, than it is to make up an answer. If you are interviewing for a position in a new career, you may consider mentioning that was not something covered in your training. Be honest about your knowledge but continue to stress your ability and willingness to learn new skills and gain new knowledge.

If a question catches you off guard, it is also alright to pause while you think it through. What may seem like an infinitely long pause to you, may actually be only a few seconds. You are, after all, the one in the hot seat. A thoughtful answer after a deliberate pause will score more points with the interview than a quick answer that does not address the deeper aspects of the question.

Handling rejection

Most often, during or after the interview, you will usually have a gut feel about how it went. If the interview was shorter than expected, or if the interviewers seemed to lose interest, repeatedly looked at their watches, or doodled on their notes, you can probably expect you will not be contacted for the next step. The decision about your fate with that company was probably made before you left the interview.

Even in these situations, when you know the rest of the interview is simply perfunctory; do not slip out of your most professional demeanor. Always remain polite and continue to do your best. In the worst case scenario, you will leave the interviewers with a favorable opinion of your professionalism. In the best case, you may be able to regain their interest and salvage the interview.

Handle all rejection graciously, in doing so you will again set yourself apart from the vast majority of other job hunters. It is customary in many cases to send a note (or email) thanking the interviewer for the chance to interview before you know the results. However, consider sending a note of thanks even after you receive notice you have not been selected for the position. In this note or letter, express sincere thanks for the opportunity to interview, acknowledge your disappointment in not getting the position if you like, but ensure you make it clear you trust their judgment. Do not beg and plead for another position. Wish the interviewer and the company well and mention that you enjoyed getting to know all the members of the interview panel.

While there is no guarantee a note of thanks after a rejection will ever lead to a position with that firm, it will certainly enhance their opinion of you. If another position opens, that favorable opinion may be enough to get you in for another interview. At the very least, if you ever run into the person who interviewed you again, you can hold your head high knowing that person knows how professional and gracious you really are.

a. It's not about you

When you are rejected for a position, try your best to see it for what it truly is. A rejection letter does not mean the interviewers are rejecting you as a person. Do not internalize not being hired as indicative of your self-worth. Doing so will continue to eat away at your already lowered levels of self-esteem.

By not selecting you, the employer simply selected someone else for the position. You were not rejected. You were just not the one they selected, this time. The individual they hired was probably just a better match for the job or the company. He or she was not a better person than you.

Try instead to focus on the positives. Finishing second in a race is certainly not the same as winning. Being interviewed and not being selected does not feel as good as being hired. However, consider the bigger picture for a moment. The very fact you were called in for an interview means you were selected from a much larger pool of applicants with qualifications very similar to yours. In some cases, the number of applicants could be in the hundreds or even more.

While not being hired after being interviewed can be a blow to your ego, it can also be a very important time to learn from the experience. First, evaluate your interview performance. Were you lacking some important skills related to the position? If so, use this as a motivation to study and enhance those skills when you can. Or, were you caught off guard by some other type of question, a lightsaber question for example? If so, you will be more ready for this type of question the next time. Practice your interview skills with family members or at a support group.

b. Ask for feedback

If you send a letter or email after receiving the notification you were not hired, you may also ask for feedback on your interview performance. Do not demand this, but ask for feedback in a gracious and professional manner. If you feel uncomfortable asking for feedback from the hiring decision maker, you may consider sending a short note or email to the one who scheduled the interview with you.

Many times, potential employers will not provide useful feedback. They may simply respond by simply stating they hired the most qualified individual. At other times, you may receive valuable feedback that you can utilize at your next interview. The valuable information you will receive when the employer does provide you with feedback makes asking for it every time, very worthwhile.

The dirty little secret

Many companies and especially some government agencies must follow strict hiring procedures. For example, they may be mandated by procedure or statute to publically advertise a position and interview the top few candidates. However, in some cases, there will be an internal or other known candidate also applying for that position. In most of these cases, the hiring decision is already made, but the interviewing process still continues.

Unless you are familiar with the company or organization where are you are interviewing, you will not know if you are competing against an internal candidate who has all but been promised the job. You may interview superbly well, make great connections with everyone on the panel, but still not be offered the job. Even if your qualifications and interviewing skills were superior, the job will most likely be offered to someone they already know if the company or agency wants that individual promoted. The result of an interview in this situation leaves you scratching your head wondering why you were not offered the position. Once again, this is not a personal rejection of you; you were simply there to ensure regulations were met.

When you receive an invitation to interview, you cannot be sure if there is already a likely candidate for the position. Do your best in every interview and try to use each one as a learning opportunity. If the interview requires travel, one possible clue to an organization already having someone in the running is their willingness to provide travel reimbursement. If they are not willing to do this, or do not do this by policy, investing your own money to travel to this interview is probably not money well spent.

If you are rejected to an internal candidate, consider the positives rather than the negatives. Sure, once again you did not receive a job offer, but the organization actually brought you in to compare with their internal candidate. In other words, they were likely going to hire the internal candidate, but they wanted to interview you just in case. This means you were as strong as, or even stronger than the internal candidate in some areas. You were interviewed to highlight the strengths and weaknesses of the internal candidate. While being hired this time may be unlikely, once again you have made contacts and you will become a known quantity for the next opening.

DOWN BUT NOT OUT

If you learn from defeat, you haven't really lost
                                                     Zig Ziglar

Key Points/Action Steps

- Prepare for the unexpected

- Never give up, even when it seems hopeless

- Handle rejection graciously

- Ask for feedback when possible

- They did not reject you. You made it near the top. They simply selected someone else.

CHAPTER SEVEN

Preparing for your next interview

When one door closes, another opens; but we often look so long and so regretfully upon the closed door that we do not see the one which has opened for us.

Alexander Graham Bell

As you have hopefully already realized, the difference between getting hired and remaining unemployed can often be as simple as your overall attitude. Remember, getting to the interview means the potential employer feels you have the needed skill set. The overall purpose of the interview is to choose the candidate who best fits the organization or agency. If you are interviewing for a position and you do not have the skills it requires, you may have embellished your résumé or the potential employer may have misread it. Otherwise, by interviewing you, in most cases the employer is convinced you can do the job. So, most often it is not skills that make or break the candidate during the interview, it is personality and attitude.

Interview survival

Your skill set gets you into the interview. If your skills are lacking, improve or replace them. You will not get an interview without the required skills.

Your attitude, however, can make or break you during the interview. Before your next interview, make sure you have already taken important and tangible steps to improve your attitude. You do not want the interview panel thinking you suffer from an "Eeyore syndrome".

To help you ace your next interview and display the best attitude possible, here are two acrostics that can help you be your BEST and back on the road to RICH. Both of these deal with your presence and attitude during the interview. You may choose to incorporate one or both of these to assist you during your next interview.

Be your B.E.S.T

Body Language

Your body language often says more about you in the interview than your words. Do your best to appear comfortable, but not disinterested. Sit up straight and avoid crossing your arms as that makes you appear unapproachable. You may consider crossing your legs, but not to the point you are leaning back in a manner that may be construed as not taking the interview seriously.

Avoid fidgeting with your pen or any papers you have with you. Keep your hands on a table or desk when possible. Do not play with your hair or adjust your glasses too often. Some experts recommend taking a bottle of water with you or accepting one that is offered to you. Taking an occasional sip of water can allow you to buy some time or relieve some nervous energy.

If possible, have someone video you during a practice interview. Examine your body language closely and look for areas you can improve. There are many resources available that

PREPARING FOR YOUR NEXT INTERVIEW

discuss important interviewing body language. For example, job listing websites like CareerBuilder.com provide excellent advice.

Enthusiasm

If you are interested in the job you are applying for, let the interviewers know that by exhibiting enthusiasm for the position. Your body language will betray your enthusiasm level, so be sure the two are congruent. You can also demonstrate enthusiasm by your energy level. If you are excited about the possibility of working for this firm in this position, approach the interview with some excitement. You can do this by arriving a few minutes early and appearing interested at all times during the interview.

Another very important way you can show your enthusiasm is by asking appropriate questions. Before going to an interview you should have thoroughly researched the company or agency. You should have some appropriate questions formulated in your mind before the interview starts. Asking pertinent questions shows you are interested enough in this position to conduct some basic research.

Appropriate questions may include specifics about the position that were not given in the job description or not discussed in the interview. You may consider asking about company strategy and goals and how this position meshes with those goals. If the company has been in the news recently, you may selectively ask some questions about current issues. You may even carefully consider questions about the longevity of this position. This not only shows interest but that you are considering this a long-term position.

Questions that are not appropriate include any related to pay, benefits, or time off. Asking these questions may leave the impression you are more interested in what the job can provide you than you are interested in how you can benefit the company. Those items may truly be your primary concern and the interviewers know that. You just do not want to make that obvious during the interview. Save these questions for the negotiation rounds.

DOWN BUT NOT OUT

Smile

Never underestimate the goodwill a simple smile can produce. Remember one of the primary selection criteria during the interview is attitude. A cheerful smile, when accompanied with eye contact, will put the entire interview panel at ease. A smile in the beginning allows you to create favorable feelings during that all important first impression. Smiling when appropriate during the interview displays that you are in control and not incredibly ruffled under pressure. Finally, smiling again as you thank all involved in the interview may cause them to forget some of your missteps during the interview itself. When all the candidates are evaluated, a pleasant smile may give you just the edge you need to nudge out the other candidate.

Think it through

The pause you take before intelligently answering an interview question always seems longer to you than the interviewers. It is much better to think before you speak than to blurt out an unintelligible or incorrect answer. A pause before a correct or appropriate answer will have far less consequences than something you say out without thinking it through.

If you are the type of person whose response to being nervous is talking very quickly, make the conscious effort to slow down. Talk slowly enough to be clearly understood, but not so slowly that you appear half asleep. Show that you are thoughtful and deliberate, but not so deliberate to be considered dull.

Taking your time also means observing your surroundings. Watch those who are interviewing looking for clues that can help you better respond to what they are looking for. Look for clues about the organization or individuals in the room. You may notice a plaque, trophy, or diploma that you can use as a conversation starter to build report with the interviewer.

The B.E.S.T method helps demonstrate the positive attitude you have been cultivating. Just remember to be aware of your body language, show enthusiasm, smile and make eye contact, and take your time answering the interview questions.

PREPARING FOR YOUR NEXT INTERVIEW

Incorporating the B.E.S.T technique at your next interview will help the potential employer know you are the perfect candidate for the job.

Make the BEST impression at your next interview!

- Body Language
- Enthusiasm
- Think it through
- Smile

The R.I.C.H model[5]

The R.I.C.H. acrostic was developed by Cheryl Larabee. Cheryl is a lecturer at Boise State University and serves on the board of directors for several companies, including serving as chairperson of the board for a publically traded electronic accessory firm. Her many years in the banking and other industries helped her develop this model, which is very useful when dealing with people in every business situation, including job interviews.

Reflective

In situations like a job interview, it is helpful to reflect the other individual's personality and body language. Being reflective of the other person puts them at ease and helps them see you in the most positive light because they see you as they see themselves.

For example, perhaps the individual interviewing you appears to be quiet and reserved. You can also detect this in the individual's body language as he or she appears to value their personal space. When dealing with a reserved person like this, reflecting those traits to the best of your ability will give a positive impression. Respect their personal space. Do not lean too far forward. If the individual is leaning away from the interview table, you may consider a similar posture. On the other hand, if the individual you are with is expressive, uses hand motions, or talks with excitement feel free to reflect their personality.

Being reflective is something that takes considerable practice, but you likely have the time for that. Being reflective does not mean mimicking or mocking the other person. It is simply a response to the clues you have been given by the other individual to put them at ease. Being reflective also puts you in the best light possible.

---

[5] © Cheryl A. Larabee, used by permission

PREPARING FOR YOUR NEXT INTERVIEW

Interested, not interesting

Many people mistakenly approach an interview from the perspective of trying to make themselves appear interesting. While it is important to do a fair amount of self-promotion during the interview, the most lasting results will come when you focus on being interested rather than being interesting.

Quite simply, one of the easiest ways to appear interested is to talk less about yourself, and by asking questions of those in the interview when possible. Again, you will have to discuss yourself during some interview questions but when given time, ask questions about the job, the organization, and those interviewing you. Often as the interview ends you will be asked if you have any questions. Use this time wisely to appear interested in the position. Ask about the company's biggest challenges and how you can help solve those problems.

Cheerful

Here is still another reminder to smile. A negative attitude has no place in the interview room. You need to ensure it stays home if you insist on keeping it around. People like to do business and work with pleasant people. One of the best ways to rise above the other candidates being interviewed is to simply be cheerful during the entire interview process, from the time you walk in the door to the time you leave.

Helpful

Use every opportunity you have to be helpful before, during, and after the interview. Being helpful can involve something as simple as holding the door open for someone as you are walking into the interview room. Or, perhaps something will come up in the interview that will allow you to be helpful. Perhaps you recently read an article that provided pertinent information. You can offer to email the article or a link to it after the interview. Something like this not only lets you display your helpfulness, it also gives you an additional contact with the potential employer.

DOWN BUT NOT OUT

Incorporating the R.I.C.H. technique may give you just the edge you need to win out over the other candidates. Just remember your use of this technique should be genuine and practiced. Ensure that you are comfortable with each aspect of this technique so that your efforts do not appear phony or contrived.

The R.I.C.H. model Remember to be...	
Reflective	Interested
Cheerful	Helpful

We shall never know all the good that a simple smile can do.

Mother Theresa

PREPARING FOR YOUR NEXT INTERVIEW

Key Points/Action Steps

- During your interview be your BEST:
    o Watch your body language
    o Show enthusiasm
    o Smile
    o Think before time answering questions

- On the road to RICH you should be:
    o Reflective
    o Interested
    o Cheerful
    o Helpful

CHAPTER EIGHT

Back to school?

Realizing you don't already know everything can be quite painful.

Luther Maddy

After honestly examining your hard and soft skills, you probably found some areas where you can improve. For example, if the hard skills you have relied on throughout your career are no longer in high demand, you either need to upgrade them or find some new ones. Soft skills can also be improved with training and education. While you may have a talent for some soft skills, those talents can be honed considerably through formal training.

After coming to the realization your skill repertoire needs enhancing, it is then time to consider your training and education options. Your options for enhancing existing skills or acquiring new ones are only limited by time and finances. Your locale was once a major limiting factor in educational opportunities, but the internet and online education have all but eliminated this for many types of education. So, no matter where you live, you will likely have several educational and training opportunities available to you. Now, you just need to decide what type of education you want to pursue and how you will pay for it.

Has your unemployment made you damaged goods?

Before discussing specific training options there is another dirty little secret you need to be aware of. While few employers will admit it publically, some do not look favorably on unemployed individuals. Résumés that reflect the applicant is currently unemployed sometimes do not make it past the initial screening, even when the individual clearly matches the requirements of the position. Likewise when individuals who fill out applications and report their date of last employment may also find their applications do not make it past the first screening.

In good economic times, there is a stigma attached to unemployment. The assumption is that layoffs are used to weed out mediocre employees. This conjecture, even though it may have nothing to do with why you were laid off, still permeates some firms. In tougher economic times, the stigma of unemployment is somewhat lessened, but a prejudice exists in many companies against those who have been unemployed for six months or longer and that can affect your chances of re-employment. The ugly fact is that some hiring professionals consider the unemployed to be damaged goods and often avoid hiring them.

The stated purpose of this book was to provide you some encouragement. The last two paragraphs probably did not meet that goal. However, there are some important things you can do to counter the prejudices that may exist against the unemployed.

First, you can account for your time during unemployment. You do not want to have a potential employer thinking you have been sitting on the couch watching soap operas and eating chocolates for the last six months. Or maybe in your case it is stock car racing and beef jerky. Instead, you want to show the potential employer that you have used your time wisely. Have you volunteered at the local food bank, rescue mission, or blood center? If so, make sure the potential employer knows that.

Second, you can show that not only did you use your time wisely, but you also used your time of unemployment to make

BACK TO SCHOOL?

yourself a better employee. Pursuing training or furthering your education while you are unemployed demonstrates drive and signifies you are open to change. It also shows a potential employer you were not content to sit home and wait for a job to come to you while you collected your unemployment checks.

People live in a world of perceptions, even when those perceptions do not match reality. As an unemployed individual may feel they are less capable than they really are due to their perceptions, employers also have perceptions about unemployed individuals. Those perceptions may be entirely baseless, but realizing they exist, you need to do everything in your power to counter those negative perceptions and you can do that through using your time wisely and perhaps pursuing further education.

> ***Note:*** *If you are receiving and relying on unemployment compensation, check with your labor department before pursuing any training or education. Federal rules have recently changed for the better, but in some cases enrolling in an educational program may cause you to lose your unemployment benefits. In some instances, your labor department may be able to help fund your training as well. Some of these funding options will be discussed later in this chapter.*

Selecting a training option

In addition to time and money, your educational choice will also be affected by your own career aspirations and existing educational attainment. The first step if pursuing further education is deciding what you want to be when you grow up. You probably thought you had already made this decision, but that was when you still had a job.

Your current situation can actually become the opportunity for you to pursue something you have always wanted to do. Perhaps you were becoming a little burned out at your previous job. Maybe you dreamed of being in a different career. Well, this may be just the chance you secretly wanted. If you were happy in your previous career and considered it your dream job, you may not need to change careers. Instead, you can use this time as an opportunity to become even better at that career. Either way, the answer is in additional training.

If you have decided to improve your existing skills or acquire new ones, the next decision is how and where. There are a myriad of schools, colleges and universities vying for your money. In return they nearly all promise to get you into a high paying job quickly and with little or no effort on your part. No doubt, if you have been unemployed for more than a few days, you have probably noticed advertisements from several different colleges and universities. And, while the "new job with the little or no effort on your part" comment was somewhat facetious, there is a wide disparity in the price and quality of education available. And, those institutions who try the hardest to get you to enroll usually have the highest costs and lowest reputations among employers in the area. Instead of choosing a training option based on television commercials, direct mailings, websites, or even personal visits, you need to do some research.

a. Career school, college, or university?

Universities, colleges, and career schools may be public or private, not-for-profit and for-profit. For example, the University of California is a public, state regulated system. Universities may also be private. Harvard, for example is a private, not-for- profit, university. Other universities, especially those that advertise heavily, are both private and run as a business and must earn a profit. The same is true for colleges and career schools.

There is nothing inherently wrong with a private or for profit educational institution. For-profit institutions pioneered quality online education which has now been embraced by many public institutions. For-profit schools have also opened satellite campuses in many areas with smaller population bases, expanding the educational opportunities available. And, schools that operate for a profit are often the first to offer training programs geared to new and in-demand careers because they can change faster than larger, entrenched academic institutions.

As with any business, there is a wide variation in both the cost and quality of for-profit institutions. Overall, for-profit schools tend to be more expensive than public institutions. Their quality can vary widely as can their tuition fees.

When choosing a college or university you may also hear the terms liberal arts and career college. Liberal arts institutions are the typical degree granting institutions and offer degrees in subjects like history, literature, as well as career oriented subjects like accounting and computer science. These colleges and universities usually focus on academic degrees at the bachelors level or higher.

Career colleges typically offer degrees that are geared to specific careers. Often the degrees offered by career colleges are associate degrees. For example, a career college may offer an associate's degree in Medical Assisting. While many career colleges are for-profit companies, you can also find career colleges operating within many public universities. Local community colleges usually offer a dual track, one track for students seeking to transfer to a four year college and another track for those seeking vocational associates' degrees.

The last category is the career or vocational school. These schools offer certificates rather than degrees. Typically their programs are shorter than two years in duration, sometimes considerably shorter. Career schools focus on specific skills that can assist in gaining employment quickly in the field of training. Many career schools are for-profit, but they can also be operated by non-profit agencies and many community colleges offer short term career oriented certificates.

A career school is also an excellent option if you simply need to enhance or refresh some existing skills. For example, if you need to learn the latest and greatest word processing, small business accounting, or spreadsheet program, there is very likely some short term training available at a local career school. Career schools can also provide enhancement in skills ranging from welding to medical coding.

    b. Choose, don't be recruited

It feels good to be wanted, especially after being unemployed and going on a few interviews and not being the one selected for the position. However, when it comes to selecting where you wish to pursue education or training, heavy handed recruiting techniques should serve as an important clue. Aggressive recruiting usually indicates the school charges more than you could pay elsewhere for similar or perhaps better training.

Recruitment is always about what you have to offer the college. And, unless you are being offered a spot on the football team, or perhaps the golf team; what you have to offer the college at this point in your life is a body in a class. Or, to put it another way, you represent money for the school. If you feel pressured to enroll quickly and are being contacted to the point it borders on harassment, you should probably look at other training options.

    c. Ask potential employers

If you are considering a career related certificate or degree, one of the best ways to evaluate the quality of a school is to talk to those that may potentially hire you after completing your training. For example, if you are thinking about enrolling in a program to become a dental hygienist, call a few dentists before signing on the dotted line. Mention that you are considering enrolling in the program and mention the institution. Ask if they hire graduates from that school. Ask what they think about the quality of education provided at that school. Maybe you are considering a computer security degree. Try contacting potential employers for this program, asking the same questions as well.

As you consider enrolling in a particular school, that school should be able to provide you with a list of employers who have hired their graduates. Call some of the employers on this list to verify this is indeed the case. But, more importantly, be sure to call some of the employers in that field of training who are not on the list. Perhaps there is a reason they do not hire that school's graduates, or perhaps leaving their name off the list was an oversight.

   d. **Ask your labor department**

The employees at your local labor department can also provide some valuable assistance in selecting training, and perhaps even provide assistance paying for that training. First, to avoid lawsuits from training vendors, your labor department counselor must usually remain neutral in your training selection, if they are providing the funding. If you are paying for your training on your own or with federal grants or loans, they will usually be more objective. As mentioned in the earlier note, it is very important that you let your labor department counselor know you are planning to further your education if you are receiving or are planning to receive unemployment compensation benefits.

   e. **Compare costs**

Public and most reputable private institutions will have their tuition costs readily available. In many cases you can find this information on their web sites or catalogs. If the school or college you are considering attending is not forthcoming with tuition prices, it probably means they are charging too much in comparison to other schools.

When you are able to get a clear cost, compare that cost to others. Some for-profit schools do charge considerably more than comparable or even better quality public colleges. Use the decision making skills you have developed to make the best choice for your particular situation.

   f. **Check accreditation**

Accreditation is an interesting and somewhat confusing concept. Accreditation affects your ability to get federal tuition assistance and loans. Accreditation can also affect your ability to transfer credits from one institution to another. To simplify this concept, accreditation can fall within three categories when it comes to making a school choice.

The most respected accreditation is regional. Schools with regional accreditation include public colleges and universities and well respected private institutions. Regional accreditation bodies include New England Association of Schools and Colleges, Western Association of Schools and Colleges, and several others. Schools with regional accreditation are eligible for federal tuition assistance, as long as the program you are enrolling in is also eligible. Credits from regionally accredited institutions will usually transfer for any other college or university, within an individual school's policies.

The second level of accreditation is national accreditation. National accrediting bodies include agencies like Accrediting Council for Continuing Education and Training, Distance Education and Training Council, and others. College credits that are earned from nationally accredited schools may be accepted by other nationally accredited schools. However, these credits are almost never accepted by colleges and universities that are regionally accredited. This means if you earn a two year degree from a nationally accredited college and then decide to pursue a four year degree from a public university, you may find that none of your previously earned credits transfer.

The third level of accreditation is no accreditation at all. While not being accredited at all may seem like it should be a deal breaker from the start that is not necessarily the case. One drawback to attending a non-accredited school or program is that you will not be able to apply federal financial aid, grants or loans, to help pay for your training. However, non-accredited schools often charge far less than their accredited competitors for the same or similar programs. If you are looking for career training only, do not intend to use that training for degree purposes in the future, and can pay for your training without federal financial aid, then attending a non-accredited school can be a very viable option.

Paying for retraining

    a. **Your state**

Funding to provide training assistance to the unemployed falls within three broad programs, the Workforce Investment Act (WIA), the Trade Adjustment Assistance (TAA), and other state funding programs. The Workforce Investment Act provides funding for skills enhancement and career retraining. This source is usually for short term training but, depending on funds availability and your career goals can sometimes be used for longer programs leading to a degree. WIA funds are divided into several categories such as youth, adult, dislocated worker, and even displaced homemaker. When funds are tight in this program, priority is given to low income clients.

Trade Adjustment Assistance training funds can provide funding for training up to 130 weeks in duration. This program is not income based but is dependent upon the circumstances of your layoff. Eligibility for this program is determined by the United State Department of Labor and is contingent on several employees losing their jobs due to a shift in production caused by trade agreements. If you are eligible for this program, your state department of labor will usually let you know.

Many, but not all states have additional programs that can provide training assistance. These are funded and administered by the individual states. The states determine eligibility and your state department of labor can provide more information about these programs if they exist in your state.

    b. **The Federal government**

Depending on the school and training program you choose, you may be eligible for two types of training assistance from the federal government, Pell grants and federal student loans. Pell grants are needs based and in addition to meeting income and asset requirements, students must also be enrolled in eligible programs at an eligible school. Eligible programs include degree completion programs and vocational training programs that are at least 600 clock hours in length. The school must also be at least nationally accredited.

Federal student loans fall into two categories, subsidized and unsubsidized. Subsidized loans, like Pell grants are needs based. Interest is not accrued while you are in school with subsidized loans. Interest is charged and accrued beginning with the date of disbursement for unsubsidized loans. Repayment of student loans usually begins six months after you complete your education. There are a variety of repayment plans and loan forgiveness programs available as well. You can find more information about these at the Department of Education website. As with Pell Grants, the availability of student loans depends on the program and school you choose.

The roots of education are bitter, but the fruit is sweet.

Aristotle

BACK TO SCHOOL?

Key Points/Action Steps

- Account for your time during unemployment
    - Volunteer
    - Get some training

- Attending training during unemployment:
    - Gives you new or enhanced skills
    - Shows potential employers you were not wasting time
    - Can build your self-image

- Choose your training option carefully
    - Check with potential employers
    - Compare costs
    - Examine accreditation
    - Use the Training Option Evaluation Form

- Choose, don't be recruited

- Explore financial aid options

Using the Training Option Evaluation form

This form is designed to assist you in the process of evaluating training options. It will not make the decision for you, but it will help you make your decision somewhat more objectively. Rather than simply going on "gut feel" or being pressured by a school recruiter, this will help you quantify some important considerations while you are evaluating different career options.

The top half of this form lets you objectively evaluate different school choices by comparing school type, accreditation, program type and cost. Remember regional accreditation is important if the program offers college credit and you envision yourself furthering your education at some point in your life. If training for a specific career is your goal, then accreditation is not as important.

The second half of the form allows you to add a numeric score to your assist with your decision. After reading each statement, place a value of 1 through 5 in the scoring box. The number you choose will depending on the scale with 1 being strongly disagree and 5 being strongly agree. As the statements are worded on this form, 1 would represent the lowest score possible and 5 the highest.

The highest score possible is 40. If you are evaluating more than one program/school choice, the total score for each should assist your decision making process.

BACK TO SCHOOL?

Training Option Evaluation form

School or college:						Total score:	
Type of school:	☐ College or University		☐ Community College		☐ Career college		☐ Vocational School
Accreditation:	☐ Regional		☐ National		☐ None or N/A		
Program of study:							
Program Type:	☐ Diploma				☐ Certificate		
Total program completion time:			Total cost of program (tuition and books):				
Expected wages after completion:							
Will this program earn college credits?			☐ Yes		☐ No		☐ N/A
If yes, will these credits transfer to regionally accredited colleges or universities?					☐ Yes		☐ No

Grading Scale	strongly disagree (1)	Disagree (2)	neutral (3)	agree (4)	strongly agree (5)

Evaluation Criteria	Score
1. Local employers hire graduates from this school and program	
2. This school and program fits my overall lifetime career goals	
3. This school and program has a good reputation with employers	
4. This school has a good reputation with career counselors	
5. The total costs are reasonable compared to other options	
6. Upon program completion, the starting wage I can expect is worth the cost of this program	
7. The placement rate for this school and program is better than other training options	
8. I do not feel pressured into choosing this school and program	
Total Score:	

CHAPTER NINE

Working outside the box

You miss 100 percent of the shots you never take.
                                            Wayne Gretsky

    Your current unemployment does not have to be the worst thing that has ever happened to you. Unemployment may be a chance for you to try something you have always wanted to do. Perhaps you have dreamed of owning your own business, or pursuing a completely different career. This may well be your chance to pursue a dream. At the very least, some of the options in this chapter may help you earn some income while you are waiting for better employment.

    Where you end up after being unemployed is truly up to you. The result of your current unemployment may be finding yourself in a position very similar to the one you most recently had. Or, you may have to invest a little time and find a new career after some additional education. Or, you may use this time to discover your true calling in life.

    Your financial reality may dictate much of your decision making processes at this point, but if you have a dream, do not let it go. Sure, you may need to get a job, any job, to pay the bills, but do not let that dissuade you from the bigger picture of doing what you do best, what you were meant to do. Tom Rath puts it this way,

> *Far too many people spend a lifetime headed in the wrong direction. They go not only from the cradle to the cubicle, but then to the casket, without uncovering their greatest talents and potential.*[6]

Use this time of self-evaluation wisely. Perhaps you are destined for huge success, or perhaps you will find yourself in a vocation you truly enjoy after unemployment.

You the boss?

If you have an idea that could be turned into a business, this may be the time to pursue that idea to the fullest. Is there something you absolutely love to do that could become a business or at least generate some income? Many very successful businesses have been started as a result of the owner's unemployment. Many of these started as home based businesses and grew into huge companies. Perhaps your idea can do that for you. Or, perhaps you will not find immense success but will find contentment in owning a business doing something you love.

Starting a business can be a relatively easy process. The next few paragraphs will give you a brief overview of some of the things you should consider when starting a business. This is not meant to be a comprehensive guide. You can find very detailed information and more assistance in some of the resources listed at the end of this section.

Your business structure

After deciding you want to start a business, one of the first decisions you need to make is how you want to structure your

---

[6] Rath, Tom, 2007 "Strengths Finder 2.0"

business. You can structure your business as a sole proprietorship, a partnership, or a corporation.

A sole proprietorship is the simplest type of business structure to select. With this structure, you and the business are the same legal entity. The ease at which a sole proprietorship can be established is one of this structure's main advantages. Other advantages include not having to share the profits with any other partners or shareholders and as the business owner, you have complete control.

One of the disadvantages of sole proprietorships includes survivability. If the owner passes away, the business legally ceases to exist. Another significant disadvantage is the lack of separation between the business liabilities and personal assets. In other words, if a sole proprietorship fails, its debts must be paid from your personal assets. Many small businesses begin as sole proprietorships and then change structure as they grow. In the United States today, most small businesses are sole proprietorships.

Partnerships involve more than one person. There is a little more work setting up a partnership than a sole proprietorship because there should be a formal partnership agreement. This agreement should spell out issues of control, handling disputes, and being able to exit the agreement. This business structure is not commonly used, but is very common in legal and accounting firms. One of the major disadvantages of partnerships is that all partners are personally responsible for partnership debts and other liabilities.

Incorporating has the advantage of limiting your personal liability as a business owner and clearly separates business finances from personal assets. There are different varieties of corporations you can establish. Corporations differ on how income or loss is taxed and how many shareholders the corporation can have. Setting up a corporation is a little more difficult than starting business as a sole proprietor. If you think a corporation is for you, you will probably want to employ the services of an attorney, or at least get some good legal advice from an expert.

Unless you have an idea for a business that you are sure will become the next technology giant, the main things to consider when choosing a business structure are the protection of your personal assets and how business income will be taxed. Since most businesses lose money in the first few years, choosing a structure that allows you to deduct those losses on your personal tax returns is probably a good idea.

The business plan

Starting a business is not something you should attempt without considerable planning. Most entrepreneurs do not simply stumble into success. A well thought out and executed plan is usually the roadmap to a successful startup. Your plan does not necessarily need to be a 40 page business plan, replete with income projections, but it should be detailed enough to guide you toward your ultimate goal.

The step by step process of starting a business is beyond the scope of this book. Fortunately, there are a myriad of excellent resources available to help you do just that. Some of those resources include:

Small Business Administration (SBA.gov)

The Small Business Administration's website is an excellent resource for those considering starting their own business. This website includes information and training on basic bookkeeping and taxes. You can also find information pertaining to the legal structure of your business.

Small business development centers

Most states have small business development centers. You can often find these tied to college campuses. Small business development centers can provide you with a wealth of information in starting and managing a business. And, in cases where a college campus is nearby, there may also be some students who may be willing to provide you with marketing or other assistance as part of a class project.

Other non-profits

There are many non-profit organizations that provide assistance to those considering starting a business. Some of these organizations provide online training and other resources. One of these is MyOwnBusiness.org. A visit to this website will provide a wealth of information for forming and managing your own small business.

While you are waiting to make money

Few businesses become wildly successful as soon as they are started. Even for the best ideas and the most dedicated entrepreneurs it takes some time before the business venture provides a living income. While you are waiting for your new business to become successful you may consider taking on a low stress full or part-time job. This can help you meet your obligations without having to drain your fledgling business of its needed capital.

Depending on your business idea and your personal financial strength, you may consider taking on a partner or investor. Some of the previously mentioned resources, like Small Business Development Centers can provide practical information about financing a business start.

Do not be defined by failure

Perhaps as your financial condition has worsened and your prospects have dimmed, you decided things can never get any better. This does not have to be the case. Adversity can be a powerful motivator and many highly successful individuals started successful businesses or switched careers after failures, including being fired or laid off. Many of these even experienced their greatest successes after hardships which even included bankruptcy for some. The key to their success is never giving up.

DOWN BUT NOT OUT

John C. Maxwell in his book *Failing Forward* sums up the concept this way:

When I was growing up, one of the questions I used to hear from motivational speakers was this: "If the possibility of failure were erased, what would you attempt to achieve?".

That seemed to be to be an intriguing question. At the time it prompted me to look ahead to life's possibilities. But then one day I realized that it was really a bad question. Why? Because it takes a person's thinking down the wrong track. There is no achievement without failure. To even employ that it might be possible gives people the wrong impression.

Here are some examples who model this spirit.

Walt Disney

Walt felt his calling in life was his artistic abilities and vision to bring other people enjoyment. He also wanted to use these gifts to earn a living. As a young man, Disney was hired by the Kansas City Star newspaper. His job there did not last long and he was fired after being told he lacked the creativity needed to work for the paper.

Determined not to give up, Disney partnered with another man to produce short films and animated advertising in Kansas City. Because of some unethical dealings of one of the firms he contracted with, Disney soon had far more bills than income in the business. The result was Disney filing bankruptcy and closing.

The defeats of being fired and going bankrupt still did not deter Disney from his dreams. After his company failed, he moved to Hollywood and continued to pursue his dreams. In California he endured additional setbacks but still pressed on toward his goal. Finally, in 1955, the culmination of his dream,

Disneyland, opened its gates. Had Disney decided to let his initial failures define him, the Disney empire would have never existed.

Harlan Sanders

"Colonel" Sanders struggled for years in his early career as he moved from job to job, getting fired now and then along the way. He then moved into perfecting his recipe for frying chicken and running a successful business. Sanders' first restaurant burnt to the ground when he was 49 years old. Refusing to give up, he rebuilt it and expanded the restaurant substantially where he served his fried chicken.

Fifteen years later, when he was 65, a new interstate freeway bypassed his restaurant. Business dried up and Sanders was sure he would soon be facing bankruptcy. Instead of being content to retire and live on his social security checks, Sanders decided to focus all of his attention on selling franchises for his chicken recipe.

Discovering his true calling later in life and after much adversity, Sanders sold the United States portion of his franchise operation for $2 million in 1964 at the age of 74. He kept ownership of the Canadian portion of his business. By the time he passed away in 1980 at the age of 90 he had given away millions of dollars to charitable causes.

Bernard Marcus

Bernard Marcus may not be a household name, but the company he cofounded is very recognizable. At a young age, Bernard planned to enter the medical profession. The son of Russian-Jewish immigrants, he quickly realized he did not have the needed money to pursue his dream of becoming a medical doctor. Instead, he paid his own way through pharmacy school by working at his father's cabinet shop.

After graduating as a pharmacist, Bernard began working for a drug store. However, he soon found he was much more interested in the retail operations of the business than he was in filling prescriptions. This interest led him into a career in business and by the time he was in his late forties he was an executive for a chain of home improvement stores.

All went well in Marcus' career as an executive for quite some time until he disagreed sharply with one of his superiors. The ultimate result of this disagreement was that Marcus, nearing the age of fifty, was fired. Also fired as a result of this same disagreement was Arthur Blank. Rather than resting on his laurels or dwelling on being fired, Marcus set out on another adventure late in life. The result of his firing and subsequent partnering with Blank is the chain of home improvement stores known as Home Depot.

Martha Stewart

Running a successful business requires making many decisions. Sometimes choosing the wrong decision can result in a severe downturn in the business, or even land the business owner in prison. This was the case of Martha Stewart, who by the time she was 60, had created an extremely successful business around her personality and creativity.

In 2001, Stewart made the decision to sell some of her stock based on information not available to the public. She avoided a loss by selling the stock before it fell in value. As a result of this transaction she was convicted of insider trading and sentenced to prison.

At the age of 63 she reported to prison to serve her time. Stewart spent a little over one year in prison and when released, was required to spend five months in what was essentially house arrest. After that, she spent a little more than one year on supervised probation.

As can be expected, Stewart's brand was damaged by her conviction and incarceration. Many people expected she would break under the strain of being locked up. Many analysts predicted the business she had spent so much time and energy on would disintegrate.

Stewart did not let a prison sentence define her. Instead of giving up and feeling like a failure, she hit the ground running after leaving prison and began rebuilding her image and her company. Stewart released new books, new products and a new foray into acting after prison. Her brand and company remain strong, primarily due to Stewart's determination and realization that one event does not have to determine an entire future.

Mark Cuban

You may recognize the name of this flamboyant billionaire from his appearances on television's *The Shark Tank* or from his ownership of the Dallas Mavericks basketball team. Obviously, Cuban found a successful career, but that was not the case at first. After graduating with a degree in business, Cuban had high aspirations and began looking for a job. At first, he tried working for a bank but soon became bored and quit. He then moved to Dallas to make it big, but the only income he could earn was tending bar. He finally landed a job in sales at a computer related retailer in the early 1980's while the personal computer industry was still in its infancy. Computers were new to Cuban and he was not particularly interested in them at first. He only took one computer class in college and paid a classmate to do his work so he could pass it.

Later realizing the potential in the computer industry, Cuban decided to become as knowledgeable as possible. He did not have a computer of his own so after selling a computer he offered to set it up for the customer. This gave him a chance to take the computer home and learn all he could. Before long he was an expert and a top salesperson at the store.

Cuban's story did not end with him continuing to be a salesman for a small computer retail store. After arguing with his manager one too many time, Cuban was fired. Just as he had after leaving college, Cuban had no job and no income. However, this time he had something new, important skills and knowledge.

Cuban did not let his firing define him. Rather than dwelling on the rejection, he began to put his new found skills and knowledge to work. As a result he founded his own computer service business in the Dallas area. As with most new businesses, this one struggled to become profitable. Undaunted by the failure of being fired or the fight to grow a business, he pressed on, determined to pursue his dream.

In just a few short years Cuban had built his computer business to the point that it was grossing $30 million in annual sales in 1990. It was then that he sold it to a much larger firm. With this success bolstering him, Cuban went on to create a firm that blended the Internet and entertainment. Cuban and his partner sold that new firm in 1995 for $6 billion[7].

Sell your expertise

Perhaps you have not had an idea for a new business start fermenting in your head for many years. Maybe you do not see yourself as a budding entrepreneur and the idea of creating a business might even frighten you. However, you may have very valuable skills or knowledge you can sell. The idea of becoming a consultant may not be something you have considered, but it may be the perfect stepping stone into a new position or even a successful business.

Consultants may work for themselves or another company who arranges opportunities for them. Consultants are not employees of the company or agency they consult with. Very likely you have encountered consultants or contractors in your previous work experience. You may also have developed opinions of consultants based on your previous encounters, and often those opinions are not very complementary. This is because consultants are often viewed as the first steps in a major company change. Perhaps you were laid off from a company due to a change that began with the recommendation of a group of consultants.

Unless you have previously had a career as a business analyst, becoming the consultant that recommends major company changes, is not the type of consultant you should aspire

---

[7] Doyle, T.C., 1999, Mark Cuban: From Neighborhood VAR To Internet Czar, CRN.com

to become. Instead, you can consult based on the skills and knowledge that comes with years of on-the-job experience. You likely know things about your company, the industry, or its machinery that few others know. You may be able to capitalize on that knowledge.

Do not think that consultants have to always be high powered people in formal business attire holding conferences in the corporate board room. If you can pull that off, great. If not, your consulting work may be more like coaching or training. For example, if you are an expert on some off-the-shelf or specialized software package, look for opportunities with your former employer and others to capitalize on that expertise. Do you have retail management experience? Perhaps you could offer some inventory management, purchasing, or merchandising assistance to a small local retailer. Do you know more about keeping your old company's production equipment running than anyone else? If so, let your former employer know that and offer your consulting services.

Your years in the workforce have given you varied skills and knowledge. Take an inventory of those and see what opportunities you may have to parlay them into some income. Once you have a few successful contracting or coaching gigs behind you, it becomes easier to locate additional opportunities. Perhaps, you may even find that using your skills and knowledge to help others has been your life's calling all along, and you may be able to turn that into a very successful business.

Pack up and leave

Economies vary by region and industry. Even when most of the country is in the midst of a severe downturn there are almost always regions or industries that refuse to take part. For example, in the most recent recession, while most of the United States faced double digit unemployment rates, some states were clamoring for workers. North Dakota, for example has experienced an incredible boom in recent years due to the oil industry. And, while many of the unfilled positions in this state worked directly with the oil industry, the influx of workers in this industry has spawned the need for many other types of employees as well.

Finding a job in an economically depressed region may require changing careers or changing locations. Packing up and starting over at or after mid-life may not be incredibly appealing, but think of it as another adventure in your life. And, moving away does not have to be a permanent situation. You may look at your move to a more prosperous region as a temporary stop gap until things improve where you currently live. You do not have to burn all your bridges before you move. But, if you do relocate, you may find you actually like your temporary home and decide to settle in for some time.

Everybody has talent. It's just a matter of moving around until you've discovered what it is.

George Lucas

Key Points/Action Steps

- Success does not come without some failures

- Unemployment could be a chance to discover what you really love

- Consider starting a business or possibly consulting

- Becoming re-employed may require relocating

CHAPTER TEN

What do you want to be when you grow up?

Every time I find the meaning of life, they change it.
                                        Reinhold Niebuhr

Not everyone relishes the idea of starting their own business. Some do it out of necessity and discover they had those talents all along. However, it is likely that a majority of people long for the security of a steady paycheck and a job that will last at least until the next downturn. If that is the camp you are in and the job prospects in your current profession are dimming, it is probably time to consider a completely different career.

Starting over in a new career is not a panacea and will not instantly place you on the road to riches. After completing a training program you will start near the bottom of the pay scale. And, for most careers you might be considering, the bottom of the pay scale may be far less than your last wage.

In addition to a steady paycheck, there may be some other strong advantages to changing careers. For instance, this may be a time for you to enter a career you have always found intriguing. Maybe a new career will give you the opportunity to tap into talents, gifts, and skills that you could not use at your previous position. Choose your new career wisely and you may be happier at work than ever before.

Drs. Les and Leslie Parrot have this to say about a career crisis:

> The word career in Latin is translated as "progress along a difficult road". In Greek, crisis is the "decisive moment". Thus, a career crisis may be thought of as a "decisive moment on a long and difficult road"[8].

You are at a crossroad in your career. Choosing the correct path may turn out to be the route to your dream job. Unemployed is not where you planned to be, but perhaps this career crisis will eventually become something you recall fondly, when you view it after reaching your ultimate goal. This is not the time to give up in discouragement but the time to press on toward the goal of a new, better career.

The United States Bureau of Labor Statistics reports that the average person changes jobs more than 11 times during their working life. Not all of those job changes represent career changes, but it is possible that many of those job changes do represent entirely different careers. You are in the midst of career crisis that may result in a career change. If that is the case, you want to ensure to find the career you will enjoy.

Taking a career assessment

You have probably taken at least one career assessment in your life. It may have been in high school or perhaps even more recently during your current unemployment. The purpose of most career assessments is to match your personality and job. Just as some soft skills lend themselves to certain personality types, so do different careers. For example, if you like working outdoors or working with people, you probably will not find great fulfillment in a back office job or working alone.

---

[8] Parrot, Leslie & Parrot, Les. 1995. *The Career Counselor*

WHAT DO YOU WANT TO BE WHEN YOU GROW UP?

The most commonly used career assessments employ personality and job categories first proposed by John Holland[9] in his Person/Environment theory. Holland determined that most people can be categorized into six personality types. Those personality types are realistic, investigative, artistic, social, enterprising, and conventional. When taking a Holland assessment one of the personality types will receive the highest score and will be that individual's dominant personality type. The other personality types will follow behind the dominant type in scoring. After taking a Holland assessment you will receive a code of either two or three letters that will represent your strongest personality types. For example, if your strongest personality traits are realistic, investigative, and conventional in order of score, your Holland code would be RI, or RIC depending on how many letters the assessment gives.

Just as people have personalities, Holland theorized that occupations also have traits that fit certain personalities better than others. Holland was able to place several thousand different careers into categories. Holland also assumed that people would be the happiest and most fulfilled when their careers matched the personality type. People who are able to find congruency between their personality and their environments will be the most satisfied and stable on those positions.

The six types Holland defined are as follows:

Realistic

If your dominant personality type is Realistic, you are a doer. You like working with your hands. You may enjoy athletics or working outdoors. You also enjoy working with tools, agriculture, or technology. You are prone to tinker with things and find enjoyment fixing things. Words that describe you if your dominant personality type is Realistic include stable, concrete, reserves, systematic, practical, athletic, ambitious, and self-controlled.

---

[9] Holland, John L. 1992. *Making Career Choices*

Some occupations lend themselves to individuals who are Realistic. Some of those jobs include athletic trainer, computer repair, medical assistant, nurse, service manager, property manager, and corrections officer. Just as people have two or three strong personality traits, so do careers. As you investigate possible new careers you will often see a two or three letter code assigned to it. The better the job matches your personality traits, the more satisfaction you will find in that career.

Investigative

If your personality is Investigative, you are a thinker. Investigative individuals like to solve problems and find enjoyment researching the solution. Investigative people enjoy learning new things either through formal education, on the job training, or on their own. Some words that describe you if you are Investigative include curious, scholarly, reserved, logical, analytical, and introspective. Some occupations that fit the Investigative personality include technical writer, auditor, computer programmer, research analyst, philosopher, theologian, and computer systems analyst.

Artistic

If the Artistic trait fits with your personality you are creative. Artistic people usually work better in less structured environments where they have the freedom to create. Words that would describe you is your personality includes the Artistic trait include creative, expressive, impulsive, independent, intuitive, and idealistic. Some occupations lending themselves to the Artistic personality include retail merchandising, wedding planner, writer, photographer, floral designer, interior designer, and public relations director.

Social

If you are strong in the Social personality trait you enjoy people and are a helper. The Social personality trait likes solving other people's problems through listening, offering advice,

WHAT DO YOU WANT TO BE WHEN YOU GROW UP?

training, or providing medical assistance. Words that describe those strong in the Social trait include generous, friendly, helpful, patient, kind, understanding, persuasive and idealistic. Some of the careers that fit the Social personality trait include medical assistant, registered nurse, real estate appraiser, career counselor, clergy person, and paralegal.

Enterprising

If your personality mix include the Enterprising trait you are likely confident and very adept at persuading and motivating others. If you are Enterprising, you likely enjoy managing others and strive hard to reach financial rewards, power and status. Many entrepreneurs are strong in the Enterprising trait. Words that may be used to describe you if you are strong in the Enterprising trait include assertive, energetic, adventurous, results oriented, ambitious, and optimistic. If you are strong in the Enterprising personality trait you will likely find career satisfaction as a sales person, retail manager, stock broker, travel agent, office manager, or attorney.

Conventional

If your personality mix includes being strong in the Conventional trait you are probably an organizer. You work well in a structured work environment and enjoy working with numbers and data systems. You are detail oriented and enjoy learning how things work. Some words that describe the Conventional trait include well-organized, accurate, detail oriented, conscientious, methodical, practical, structured, and efficient. If you are strong in the Conventional, trait some of the best careers for you include bookkeeper, computer operator, credit analyst, administrative assistant, records clerk, and cost accountant.

Assessing your personality

By simply looking over the list of six personality traits and their descriptions you probably have a very good idea of where you fit. However, if you would like to take an actual assessment there are several available free on the Internet. It is also very likely that your labor department has free career assessment tools available to you. Other websites you may try include:

http://www.123test.com/holland-codes-career-tests/

http://www.roguecc.edu/counseling/hollandcodes/test.asp

Considering a new career

After you have taken a good look at your personality trait mix, you should then take a closer look at the list of careers you find interesting. Just as your personality has a two or three letter code indicating dominant traits, occupations have the same two or three letter codes. According to the Holland personality / environment, the closer the occupation code matches your personality code, the more satisfaction you will achieve. However, realize there is much more to a career than its code. For instance, both sports director and funeral director have the same three letter code, (ESR). Start with the occupation's code but definitely research all aspects of a career so you do not end up in a career that does not interest you.

A great place to research potential careers is the Occupational Information Network database. This is a free site that provides considerable information about potential careers. This site allows you to search occupations by their three letter code. For example, if your personality code is RIS, you can search for occupations that match that personality code. You can access this online database at:

http://www.onetonline.org/

After you have identified your personality code and then narrowed down some new career possibilities, try using the *career change evaluation* form to help you in your decision making process.

WHAT DO YOU WANT TO BE WHEN YOU GROW UP?

New Career Evaluation						
Occupation / Job:						
Occupation code:			Your Holland code:			
	Grading Scale	strongly disagree (1)	Disagree (2)	neutral (3)	agree (4)	strongly agree (5)
	Evaluation Criteria				Item Score	
This career/occupation is in demand in my local area.						
The career/occupation is immune to business cycles and downturns.						
The pay level for entry level positions in this career is desirable.						
The career/promotion path in this occupation is compatible with the time I plan to remain in the workforce.						
I can get the education or training I need for this career in a reasonable amount of time.						
Any training or education required for this position is readily available in my area.						
This occupation has a desirable working environment.						
I would enjoy working in this occupation.						
					Total Score:	

Using the Career Change Evaluation form

This form is designed to assist you in the process of evaluating new career options. It will not make the decision for you, but it will help you make your decision somewhat more objectively. Rather than simply going on "gut feel", this will help you quantify some important considerations while you are evaluating different career options.

After reading each statement, place a value of 1 through 5 in the scoring box. The number you choose will depend on the scale with 1 being strongly disagree and 5 being strongly agree.

DOWN BUT NOT OUT

As the statements are worded on this form, 1 would represent the lowest score possible and 5 the highest.

Specifically, statement #5 assumes the career choice requires additional training. If you can transition into this occupation without any additional training, score this item with a 5 and move on the next item.

To score this potential occupation, add up all the values for each statement. The highest score possible is 45. If you are evaluating more than one career path, the total score for each should assist your decision making process.

The scoring on this career change evaluation form uses a simple total. None of the statements are assigned weights higher than any other. However, statement #8, "I would enjoy working in this occupation" is the most important statement on the form. If it were assigned a weight, it should count more than all the other statements combined. If you would not enjoy working in a particular career at all, do not even consider it. Life is too short to invest time and money to pursue a career you will not enjoy. However, if you are evaluating a couple of occupations, comparing the enjoyment factor of both, along with the other criteria should help you reach a decision.

The people who get on in this world are the people who get up and look for the circumstances they want, and, if they can't find them, make them.

George Bernard Shaw

WHAT DO YOU WANT TO BE WHEN YOU GROW UP?

Key Points/Action Steps

- People's personalities can match specific jobs

- The most satisfied people will be in an occupation that matches their personality.

- Evaluate potential new careers thoughtfully

CHAPTER ELEVEN

Some careers to consider

When your values are clear to you, making decisions becomes easier.

Roy E. Disney

So, you have evaluated all the other options and you think changing careers is your best course of action. Of course, you have taken some career assessments and have some idea of the career that might provide you enjoyment and, most importantly, some income. As you are looking at all the possible career paths that match your personality, reality is certainly going to set in.

Perhaps you can envision yourself performing brain surgery. You can handle the stress. You have steady hands and enjoy tinkering with things. And, you could certainly enjoy the income your new career as a brain surgeon would provide. But, as reality sets in, you realize you only have a few college courses under your belt. By the time you invested the fifteen years it takes to become a neurosurgeon, your hands may not be as steady as they are now.

Choosing a new career at this stage in your life will depend on your age, current financial situation, and educational background. You probably do not want to wait 15 years before you start your new job. Instead, you probably want to get trained to start a new job as quickly as possible. If you are like most people, you will probably want to go from unemployed to employed in your new career in two years or less, hopefully at lot less.

To help you evaluate your new career choice, the following few pages list some of your options. This section will be broken down into two sections. One section will list some options if you already have a college degree and another section if you do not.

If you have a college degree

A college degree can open doors, as long as it is in the right field. Degrees in basket weaving or Welsh literature of the 1950's may not find as many doors open to them as slightly more practical degrees like electrical engineering, business, social work, or even graphic design. However, even a degree in basket weaving can be beneficial when changing careers. Here are some options you can consider:

Get a master's degree

Many masters' degrees can be earned in a year or just slightly longer. Earning a master's degree can definitely set you apart from the majority of unemployed. Approximately only 8% of the United States population have masters degrees. And, the unemployment rate among those with master's degrees is significantly lower than the general population.

Before you rush out and enroll in a basket weaving master's degree program, realize that may not be the best choice. If your bachelor's degree has not caused employers to clamor for your attention, a master's degree in the same field may not greatly improve your employment prospects. Once you have a bachelors' degree, you can often earn a master's degree in a different, more in demand field. You may have to take a few foundational classes to give you some knowledge of the field, but this can usually be accomplished in one or two semesters. For example, many colleges and universities offer Masters of Business Administration (MBA) programs for people with degrees in all fields.

SOME CAREERS TO CONSIDER

Teach

If you have ever considered teaching as a career, this may be the time to pursue that dream. If your degree translates into a subject taught at the high school level i.e. English, History, Science, Math, Business, etc... it may be quite easy to transition back into the classroom, but this time as a teacher. Some states have programs that allow individuals with degrees in high demand topics like science and math to teach at the same time they are taking foundational education classes. If such a program is not available, you can usually earn a teaching certification by taking classes for approximately one year.

The demand for teachers ebbs and flows and can vary greatly in different locations. The demand for teachers is also greater in fields that traditionally pay higher outside the teaching field, like science and math. If you want to put your basket weaving degree to use as a teacher, you will probably have to search for some time, but you may be able to find one.

There are many benefits to the teaching career field, if you have the temperament. First, while you may work very hard during the school year, there is usually several weeks to recover, with pay, during the summer. Secondly, teaching can be very rewarding, which is often why individuals choose this career in the first place. And, if you are willing to teach in an underprivileged, rural or urban area, there are student loan forgiveness programs that may forgive some or all of your student loan indebtedness.

If you are interested in teaching at the middle or high school level, get in touch with your state's teacher certification office. They can provide you with specific requirements to become a teacher. They should also be able to direct you to where you can find the education classes you might need before you can be certified. You may also be able to find much of this information with a quick visit to your state's website.

In addition to teaching high school, you may also consider teaching at the college level. In most subject areas teaching college requires a master's degree in the subject area or above.

There are some professional technical fields that only require bachelors' degrees. College teaching jobs are sometimes hard to break into at the full-time level. Before becoming a full-time college instructor, you may have to break in by teaching a class or two. Once the college is familiar with you, they may consider hiring you full-time. If there are several colleges in your area, you can also teach part-time for more than one. This is a difficult way to make a living, but if you are willing to work at it, this method can provide a nice income and perhaps pave the way for fulltime employment with a college at some point.

If you do not have a college degree

Do not despair if you do not have a college degree. There are many new career opportunities that require an associate's degree or less. Some new careers you may consider require very little training. Several of these will be explained in the next few paragraphs.

Since it is always beneficial to build upon existing skills, experience and education if you have some college already completed, you may want to consider completing your degree, especially if that degree is in a field currently in demand. Many colleges have degree completion programs. Some of these offer accelerated programs to help you quickly get the credits you need to graduate. If you choose this route, be sure to select your college carefully using the guidelines covered in that section of this book.

Teach without a degree?

Many community colleges have divisions that specialize in career oriented training. The programs in these divisions are often called professional/technical programs. Specific programs might include trades like welding, auto repair, administrative assistant, or even truck driving. If you have considerable experience in a professional or technical field and enjoy sharing your knowledge with others, you may consider exploring teaching opportunities at your local community college.

SOME CAREERS TO CONSIDER

Unlike programs that offer college credit, professional technical programs usually offer certificates rather than diplomas upon completion. To teach in career oriented professional/technical programs teachers must be knowledge in their field and need to have worked a certain number of years in the field. The certification to teach these courses is usually called a vocational certificate. The specific requirements vary from state to state, so check with your state department of education and the school you are interested in teaching for to learn the requirements.

Note: The careers detailed here will include an interest (Holland) code after the job title. This is the environment code discussed in the choosing a career chapter. As that chapter stated, the most satisfied people in their careers usually are in jobs that match their personalities. Pay attention to the code as you evaluate a potential career. Remember also to include the code when you use the Career Change Evaluation form. Also, the wages reported are median wages. Median wages occur exactly between the highest and lowest wage and the ones reported are for 2012. Starting wages for a person new to a career will be less than the median in all but the most unusual circumstances.

Medical careers

If you are reading this section you have probably already ruled out becoming a brain surgeon. However, if you are still interested in this field, there are several careers in this area that are in demand and require far less than 15 years of training to get hired. Here are just a few of the careers in this field that are in demand. If this field interests you, there are several other careers you can explore on your own.

DOWN BUT NOT OUT

Registered Nurse (SIC)

Median Wage: 31.48

Registered nurses are in high demand and the outlook is bright for the foreseeable future. Currently a majority of registered nurses working today have only an associate's degree. While many colleges seem to be phasing out two year nursing programs, there are many available. If this career sounds interesting, consider a two year program to get you into the workforce quickly.

Surgical Assistant (CSR)

Median Wage: 19.57

Like nurses, surgical assistants assist doctors in surgery. This career is projected to remain in high demand. You can receive a certificate in this career in one year or less.

Medical secretary (CS)

Median Wage: 15.07

If you want to work in the growing medical field but are not thrilled with providing patient care then you might consider becoming a medical secretary. You can receive enough training to get hired in this field in just a few months.

Technical careers

Technical careers, like most other occupations are cyclical. However, openings in this field remain some of the strongest around. Working in a technical career does not mean you must work for a technical company. Every large employer needs technical employees to keep their business or agency running. Some occupations in this field are compensated very well and can be obtained after a relatively short training period. Here are a few you may wish to consider.

SOME CAREERS TO CONSIDER

Computer Network Support Specialist (REC)

Median Wage: 28.41

If you like keeping things working at their best and have a knack for technology, this may be the job for you. In this occupation you will analyze and evaluate network systems and perform maintenance. The qualifications for this position will vary by industry or agency. Often, in addition to a basic background in computer technology, industry certifications are required. Training for this position can take from several months to two years.

Computer User Support Specialist (RIC)

Median Wage: 22.32

This position works with technology but with the goal of solving the problems encountered by users. In this position you may assist users in person or over the phone. This position may also involve training users. You can be trained to enter this profession in several months or take up to two years to earn an associate's degree.

Computer Programmer (IC)

Median Wage: 35.71

Computer programmers may create the code behind anything from a smartphone application to a video game. As technology continues to change, programmers should continue to be in high demand. A bachelor's degree is usually required to become employed as a computer programmer

Other career fields

Despite tough economic times, there are many in-demand careers in construction and other trades. A few minutes of research on the onetonline.org website will steer you to many interesting career choices with a strong future outlook. Many of the careers in these fields require very short training times and offer fairly high rates of pay. You should note that some careers in the trade fields require an apprenticeship in which you receive a lower pay rate while you are being trained.

DOWN BUT NOT OUT

Tractor Trailer Operator (RC)

Median Wage: 18.37

Truck driving may require driving cross country or short distances. The forecast for truck driver openings is strong for the foreseeable future. Becoming a truck driver requires training and state licensure. You can receive the training you need to become a truck driver in just a few weeks.

Make your decision wisely. Choosing a new career is an important decision. Realize that life is too short to be miserable in a job you do not like, so choose your new career based on more than money or a quick training time. Ending up in a job you cannot stand may mean you start the process over again. Consider finding a career that matches your personality and use the Career evaluation form to evaluate alternative occupations.

It is also very important not to make a decision that will impact the rest of your life when you are feeling emotionally low. Granted, being unemployed does not contribute to you feeling cheerful, but your emotions will still ebb and flow. Make your important decisions when you are feeling your best, not your worst.

Robert Schuller summed up this important concept by saying,

> *"Never cut a tree down in the wintertime. Never make a negative decision in the low time. Never make your most important decisions when you are in your worst moods. Wait. Be patient. The storm will pass. The spring will come."*

CHAPTER TWELVE

When the wolves are at the door

I'm either going to go completely mental, completely bankrupt, or have the best success of my life.

Katy Perry

A protracted period of unemployment can devastate your finances. You may have used your savings to keep your business afloat, hoping it would turn around. Or, perhaps you used it to keep up on your house payment and other obligations. Perhaps you have exhausted your savings and have been selling items to make your monthly payments. Eventually, unless things turn around and you find a job or your business picks up, you will be completely out of funds with no way to keep up.

One of the indications of the toll of unemployment and difficult economic times have on unemployed individuals is the number of personal bankruptcy filings. From 2007 to 2010, the number of personal bankruptcy filings nearly doubled (850,912 to 1,593,081[10]) in the United States overall. Regions that were particularly hard hit by the great recession saw much greater increases. For example, in the relatively small state of Idaho the

---

[10] USCourts.gov, Bankruptcy Statistics

number of personal bankruptcies increased from 2,931 to 8,355[11] in the same time period, an increase approaching 300%. For some, bankruptcy is an easy out of their financial obligations. For others, the prospect of bankruptcy is an ugly reality as they watch their length of unemployment grow and their financial assets shrink.

If your expenses are greater than your current income or your income in the foreseeable future, you will need to make some very difficult decisions. You will also need to take a realistic look at your financial condition. This will likely include making some adjustments to your lifestyle. The steps you take right now will determine what, if anything of value you have left after you have survived your career crisis.

Examine and adjust expenses where possible

If your current monthly expenses exceed your income, you are in more than a career crisis; you are also in a financial crisis. A financial crisis calls for drastic action to keep it from becoming a disaster. A crisis is only temporary. A disaster however, may still be only temporary, but with considerable longer consequences.

One of the first things you need to do is create a monthly income statement. This statement will list all your income sources and all of your expenses. This will give you an exact monthly shortfall amount. From here, you can evaluate options to eliminate or at least lessen the shortfall. Use the form at the end of this chapter to evaluate your current financial condition.

After listing and categorizing your monthly expenses you can then see where you can possibly make some adjustments to survive this crisis. The first place to look and the easiest to trim is the discretionary category. You may be able to substantially trim your expenses by trimming or cutting trips to see your favorite barista or chef, even if that chef is a clown, king, or a guy with a giant white ball for a head. Trimming your food budget can be

---

[11] USCourts.gov, Bankruptcy Statistics

relatively easy though it may mean eating that plate of "rice and beans" financial guru Dave Ramsey is so fond of recommending.

Another area where you may be able to trim discretionary spending is your entertainment spending. Giving up cable or satellite television may seem like cruel and unusual punishment, but if it means being able to keep your home and credit rating; it could certainly be worth it. You may also want to take a good look at your cell phone plan. This may also be a place to shave a little and if that is all you need, that could make a big difference.

Consider asset modification

If you are like many unemployed Americans your monthly shortage is more than a few lattes short. If trimming your discretionary expenses is not enough to meet your expenses you will then have to look at some other options to reduce your monthly outflow. One of the categories to examine closely is the payments you are making on secured assets.

Secured assets are items that you own partially and the bank or finance company owns the rest. In other words, these are items like your car or house. You technically own the asset, but the bank who loaned you the money has a right to it if you stop making your payments.

In evaluating your secured assets, the all-important word is equity. Equity is the difference between what the asset is worth and what you owe on it. For example, assume you just purchased a new car for $30,000 and financed the entire amount. From the very moment you drive it off the lot, that vehicle decreases in value and will continue to do so as long as you own and use it. So, assume it is now worth $26,000. The equity in that vehicle is -$4,000. If you sold it for what it was worth, you would essentially have to pay $4,000 of your own money to pay off the bank and get the title.

For most of history real estate has been an appreciating asset. With an appreciating asset, you could count on the value going up over time, giving you equity above and beyond the difference between the original purchase price and the loan balance. For example, assume you purchased your home 10 years ago for $100,000 and financed the entire amount. After making payments for 10 years, your loan balance you be approximately $84,000. But, if the value of that house has increased to $120,000, your equity is $36,000, not $16,000 because of its appreciation.

During the great recession, real estate values, like cars, depreciated. This situation left many home owners with negative equity in their houses, if they had purchased during real estate's peak. If you are a homeowner, you will need to estimate your home's value to compute your equity.

Now that the accounting lesson is over and you understand equity, it is time to take a close look at the equity in your financed assets with the idea of making ends meet at the end of the month.

Vehicles are much easier to sell or finance than houses. So, if you are making car payments, this is the first thing to examine. Remember again that your current situation is temporary. Your goal is to make it through to re-employment with as little long term financial damage as possible. So, this means you may need to divorce yourself emotionally from your vehicle if it is in your financial interest to do so. You can purchase another car after you become re-employed. Doing that is much easier than losing your home to foreclosure or almost everything else through bankruptcy.

So, if you have equity in your vehicle you may consider selling it and using the proceeds to buy something else. Sure, your temporary vehicle may not be as nice as your current one, but all it needs to do is get you to an interview now and then. After all, you do not have a job to go to every day right now.

As you are evaluating the impact your vehicle is having on your monthly expense register, you may also want to carefully examine the loan balance. If your vehicle is due to paid off in a few months, you may consider cutting back in other areas to balance your budget until it is paid off. You may also consider using another asset to generate the funds you need to pay off your vehicle loan. Perhaps you do need that boat, camper, or motorcycle as much as you think. Selling another asset may allow you to pay off your car loan and keep your vehicle. And, since this situation is only temporary, you can replace the other toys after you become re-employed.

Now it is time to examine your home, if you are a homeowner. If you have equity in your home and can continue to make your mortgage payments, then the best thing you can do with your home's equity is leave it alone for now. It may come in very handy later.

If you have equity in your home you want to protect it. You do not want to your lose house and your equity in it through foreclosure. The only way to protect your home's equity is to continue to make payments. You may be able to work with your lender to re-finance or lower the interest to make the payments more affordable, but as soon as you start missing payments, you are in danger of losing both your home and the equity in it.

During your current financial difficulty you need to assume your situation will quickly turn around. However, you need to approach your finances as if this may become a protracted period of financial difficulty. Doing this will allow you to minimize the damage to your credit rating and protect certain financial assets.

Missing your first payment

Hopefully, you were able to cut some of the discretionary items from your budget or reduce your car payment and will be able to skip this section altogether. If not, then you are facing the agonizing prospect of missing a payment on one or more of your monthly obligations. This can be especially difficult when you have spent your entire life building up an excellent credit rating by paying your obligations on time, every time.

When there is more month than money you must make the decision to let some of your bills go unpaid. Choosing the correct payments to skip can make a big difference in your overall financial condition once this crisis is over. Simply put, the payment or payments you choose to skip should be unsecured debts.

Unsecured debts include medical and dental bills, credit cards, and signature loans. And, to minimize the financial damage there is a hierarchy you might consider once you realize you are going to have to leave some bills unpaid.

a. Medical/Dental Bills

If you have to reduce your monthly payments the first category to consider are medical and dental bills. If you are currently making payments to your doctor, dentist, or hospital, you may be able to negotiate lower payments. Give them a call and explain your temporary financial setback. Explain that you do intend to pay your bill in full, but your time of unemployment is making this very difficult.

As long as you are showing a good faith effort to pay your bill, most of the creditors in this category will be very understanding. You may even arrange to make very small payments until things improve. You do not want to destroy the relationship you currently have with your doctor or dentist because you may become ill while you are unemployed. You do not want to be refused medical assistance because you are not paying your existing debts.

Making arrangements with your medical and dental providers may give you enough breathing room to make ends meet each month. This may help save your credit rating and help you make good on your other debts. When things turnaround quickly, you can raise your monthly payment amount and get these paid in full.

b. Credit Cards

While your doctor or dentist may not report to national credit bureaus, your credit card companies certainly will. Missing only one credit card payment will damage your credit rating and may result in higher interest rates for that credit card at the very least. If you had no medical bills to skip or skipping them did not sufficiently reduce your monthly outflow, the next step is to stop making credit card and other unsecured loan payments.

Although it may feel like it, missing a few credit card payments is not the worst case scenario. Yes, your credit will be damaged and your interest rates will increase. But, missing a few payments is something you can easily overcome when things turn around. Missing payments on any obligation is not something to be done lightly. The damage this causes to your credit rating could be long lasting. This is something that should be done only as a last resort.

The money you do not send to your credit card companies should not fund your next vacation. That money should be used to make the payments on your secured assets such as your car loan and mortgage. If you can squeak by or are close to squeaking by, consider calling your credit card companies and ask for a hardship repayment plan. As long as you have enough income to make these payments, doing so is far better than the alternative.

If you have available credit on some credit cards resist the temptation to borrow from one to pay the other. If you cannot make your payments after adjusting your expenses and selling the assets you can, it is better to miss some payments than to worsen your debt load. Borrowing money to pay your current monthly obligations may be appealing, but it is a trap that becomes very difficult to escape, even when things turn around for you financially.

The only way you will succeed in your current financial situation is to act as if you will be unemployed for a long time in the future. Expect the best, but plan for the worst. Then, once you are reemployed, your financial house will be in order and you may be even better off than you were before unemployment.

c. **Vehicle and other secured asset loans**

Hopefully you can skip this section. However, if your income before unemployment was substantial and, if you are like most Americans, your debt load probably matched your income level. Your current income may not even be close to what you need each month. If so, it is now time to look at your secured loans. However, before you get to this point, ensure you have already adjusted the assets you were able to, paid off what you could, negotiated with your understanding creditors, and stopped making payments on your unsecured loans. If after taking those steps, you are still unable to pay your secured loans, your financial situation is getting a little more serious, but you already knew that.

Since you still have the vehicle and other items you are making payments on, it is safe to assume you have negative equity in those items. If you do have equity, go back and read the asset modification chapter. So, selling your boat, motorcycle and ATV might not be an option at the moment.

As soon as you decide to stop making payments on a secured loan, your bank or finance company will decide they can take better care of that item than you can. After you miss a few payments, receive several collection calls and several letters demanding payment, someone will contact you and kindly ask to borrow your car, truck, motorcycle, or boat. Should you rebuff their request, they might not even ask the next time they want to borrow your car.

If you are at this point, you must decide which of the items you are making payments on you can live without. If you can identify a likely candidate, stop making payments on that item and continue making payments on all the other secured assets you can. When the repossession call comes, hand over the keys with a smile. After all, you decided what you wanted to give up and the person driving the tow truck is just trying to earn a living so he can keep making his own boat payments.

Like every other financial decision you are making at this point, deciding to stop making payments on anything is a very serious decision. Despite the treatment of it in the last paragraph, it is not something to be approached lightly. Repossession is not a panacea and does not relieve you of your obligation. After a secured asset is repossessed, you may still be liable for much of the loan balance.

After a vehicle or other secured asset is repossessed, the bank or finance company sells it to recoup the loan balance. When the finance company sells a reposed vehicle, they rarely get a retail price for the item. Instead, the item is often auctioned off at a wholesale price. If the item sells for less than what you owed the finance company, and it probably will or you would have sold it yourself, you are liable for the difference. So, if you owed $10,000 on your car and the finance company sold it for $5,000, you are liable for the other $5,000. Yes, you reduced your debt by $5,000 but still owe the money but do not have the car. When your financial situation improves, the finance company will certainly remind you of your obligation. If you can continue to make your secured asset payments, make them.

d. Your home loan

If you followed the realtor's advice, you bought as much home as you could afford. Making the payments would not be a problem. Your mortgage payment would become more and more affordable as the years ticked by and your pay raises compounded. Your job or business was going great so you did not even think twice before you signed all those papers at the title company. That huge home was yours. And now so are those huge house payments.

If you are reading this section, then you are probably wondering how you are going to make those house payments. Perhaps you have already skipped a few payments or have perhaps been unable to make any payments.

Examine the equity in your home. If it is positive, consider selling it and either downsizing or renting for a while until things turn around. If your equity is negative, and you want to rid yourself of the payments, still consider talking to a realtor, just not the one who talked you into this house. You may still be able to sell your home and not be liable for any shortfall between its current value and your mortgage amount.

If you are able to make only one of your many payments, and you wish to stay in your home, make sure the one check you write each month goes to your mortgage company. Continuing to make the payments ensures you will be able to stay in your home. If you have equity in your home, continuing to make the mortgage payments protects that equity. And, as you have watched your savings and many other assets disappear, your home's equity is something worth protecting. If at all possible, continue to make your mortgage payments.

 e. Student loans
While you may end up with some student loans if you decide to pursue training for a new career, hopefully you were not making student loan payments for past training that did not keep you employed. Regardless, if you are making student loan payments, contact your loan servicer and explain your temporary financial condition. You may be able to work out a deferment plan or at least a payment reduction. Student loan obligations stay with you until the grave. Even if your condition worsens and you end up filing for bankruptcy, student loan obligations are very rarely discharged. So, since you are going to have to pay them off anyway, you might as well keep making the payments if you can.

 f. IRS or your state
If you are reading this book because of a business failure then it is not hard to envision you may owe the IRS some back payroll or other taxes. Like student loans, IRS obligations never disappear. That said, it is very likely you can negotiate a repayment plan with the IRS yourself or through a third party if you desire. If you are already on a repayment plan, continue making your agreed payments. Stopping these payments could result in the IRS seizing your assets, perhaps even including your home's equity.

g. **How about insurance?**

Vehicle insurance can keep you from losing everything you have left if you are in an accident determined to be your fault. It can also help repair or replace your vehicle after an accident, storm damage, or even vandalism. If you are making payments on your vehicle, keeping that insurance is required by your bank and they will dictate the coverage. And, unless you live in New Hampshire, you are required to have it to drive your vehicle. In New Hampshire you will still be held personally liable for causing an accident.

You probably have not even considered dropping your vehicle insurance, but you may have considered dropping collision or comprehensive coverage if your vehicle is paid for. This may save a few dollars each month, but what if your car is vandalized and all your windows are shattered while you sleep. Or, a tree branch falls on your car. Can you afford to gamble with your means of getting to work when you do find a job? Unless you have a few spare vehicles lying around, you should definitely consider keeping your insurance.

If you are making life insurance payments, you should try to continue doing so if at all possible. If you have been making term life policy payments for a few years, the rate you have now will likely be far less than payments on a new policy now that you are even a few years older. Life insurance is not for you, it is for those you love. Life insurance is not something you plan to use, but if you get hit by lightning on the way to a job interview, your life insurance proceeds can help provide for lost income and other expenses resulting from your tragic demise. If at all possible, continue to make monthly payments to your life insurance company.

Going bust

Expecting the best but planning for the worst should help you avoid reading this section completely. However, if things do not turn around quickly and your prospects are looking dim, you may be thinking bankruptcy is the only way out. Just as missing your first credit card, vehicle, or mortgage payment leads to serious consequences, bankruptcy should be your absolute last resort.

Bankruptcy does not simply wipe out all your debts and let you start over. It damages your credit far greater than missing a few payments. Bankruptcies can stay on your credit report for up to 10 years. Bankruptcies may cause your auto insurance rates to increase. It will prevent you from even applying for some jobs and may show up in a potential employer's background check before your job offer.

Financial guru Dave Ramsey has this to say about bankruptcy:

> *Bankruptcy is not something I recommend any more than I would recommend divorce. Are there times when good people see no way out and file bankruptcy? Yes, but I will still talk you out of it if given the opportunity. Few people who have been through bankruptcy would report that it is a painless wiping-clean of the slate, after which you merrily trot off into your future with a fresh start. Don't let anyone fool you. I have been bankrupt and have worked with the bankrupt for decades and it is not a place you want to visit.*
>
> *Bankruptcy is listed in the top five life-altering negative events that we can go through, along with divorce, severe illness, disability and the loss of a loved one*[12].

Much of what you are going through right now may seem beyond your control. You did not choose to be unemployed and months behind on your bills. If your re-employment prospects are not completely bleak at the moment, getting back on track and even negotiating with some of our creditors is a real possibility once you are re-employed. Bankruptcy should be the last and

---

[12] Ramsey, Dave. 2007. The Total Money Makeover

final option. It should not be approached lightly, but if your financial condition is causing you undue stress, even threatening your mental stability and your job search efforts, you may consider getting some good legal advice.

You likely never planned to even consider bankruptcy. You did not set out to purposely leave your debts unpaid. However, bankruptcy laws were enacted for people facing severe financial hardship, often due to no fault of their own. Massive medical bills, a sudden loss of income, or business failure are why bankruptcy laws exist.

Before you seriously consider bankruptcy, seek guidance from a competent attorney. You may also consider financial counseling before examining bankruptcy, but financial counseling does not work well if you have no or very little income compared to your income in the past and the debt level you have amassed. An attorney who specializes in bankruptcy will explain the options and, of course, his or her fees.

If bankruptcy is imminent, here are some things you will want to consider. First, depending on the chapter of bankruptcy you file, your unsecured debts will either be discharged or placed on an affordable repayment plan. This will include the balance you may owe after a repossession or foreclosure.

Bankruptcy laws vary from state to state but in many cases you will be able to keep as least some of the equity in your home. This fact should reiterate again how important it is to continue making your mortgage payment if you can. Another asset you may be able to keep after bankruptcy is your retirement account, such as an IRA or 401k. And, depending on the chapter filed, you may be able to keep other assets such as a vehicle, furniture, and appliances. Your attorney can provide you with exact details.

Disclaimer: The information in this chapter is anecdotal and provided for informational purposes only. It may not be applicable at all in your specific situation. This information is not intended to be a substitute for competent legal or financial council.

DOWN BUT NOT OUT

Using the financial worksheets

These worksheets are designed to allow you to evaluate your current financial situation. Worksheet A allows you to list all your sources of income. The total on this form is the money you have to work with each month to pay your bills and live on while you are waiting to become re-employed. As you fill this out, include every regular source of income you receive each month. After totaling up all income, record the total at the bottom of Worksheet A and on the top line of Worksheet E.

Next, on Form B, include the payments you are currently making on all your secured loans. If you are renting rather than buying a house, include your rent payment here. Be sure to include all payments you are making on secured assets. Include any recreational vehicle and "toy" loans here too. These are items that can be repossessed or foreclosed on if you quit making these payments. If you are renting and stop paying your rent, the eviction process is usually shorter than a foreclosure process. After listing all your secured loan payments, add them up and place the total monthly amount at the bottom of this form.

Then, use Form C to list all your non-secured loans. These include credit cards, personal loans, and payday loans for which you are currently making payments. After listing all of these, place the total at the bottom of this form.

Next, you will need to complete Form D. On this form you should list all other regular payments you are making. This will include things like student loans, child support, and even other regular payments like your insurance premiums. After listing all of your other regular payments here, total them up and enter that amount at the bottom of this form.

Now you are ready for Form E. To complete this form, ensure the total from Form A is on the top line. Then, add the totals of all your regular expenses from Forms B, C, and D. Place the total of these three forms on the second line. Finally, subtract the total regular expenditures from the income on the first line. Place the result of your calculation at the bottom of Form E.

Financial worksheets

A. Monthly Income (after taxes)	
Unemployment	
Family/Spouse Income	
Business Income	
Interest Income	
Other:	
Other:	
Other:	
Other:	
Total monthly income (A):	

B. Secured Loan Payments	
Home Mortgage or rent	
Car Payment #1	
Car Payment #2	
Other :	
Other:	
Other:	
Other:	
Other:	
Total secured payments (B):	

C. Non-secured Loan Payments

Credit Card:	
Credit Card:	
Credit Card:	
Gas Card:	
Retail Card:	
Retail Card:	
Medical/Dental	
Other:	
Other:	
Total non-secured payments (C):	

D. Other Monthly Obligations

Student Loans	
Child Support	
IRS/State	
Insurance	
Auto	
Life	
Health	
Utilities	
Auto Expense	
Other:	
Total other obligations (D):	

WHEN THE WOLVES ARE AT THE DOOR

E. Remaining monthly funds	
Total Income (A):	
Total fixed expenses (B + C + D)	−
Available Monthly	=

Spending what's left

The amount at the bottom of Form E is the money you have to live on. These forms have not completed your monthly budget. That includes things like food, entertainment, savings, and many other items. If the amount at the bottom of Form E is positive and large enough to complete the remaining items in your monthly budget, you have avoided a financial crisis and are only dealing with a career crisis.

If the amount at the bottom of Form E is negative, or not nearly large enough to meet your requirements, you are in a financial crisis as well as a career crisis. If this is the case, you will have to make some difficult decisions. Read this chapter again to help you decide which obligations will have to take a lower priority and seriously consider getting some competent financial advice to get you through this crisis.

Even cowards can endure hardship; only the brave can endure suspense.

Mignon McLaughlin

Key Points/Action Steps

- Do an honest assessment of your current financial situation

- Cut what you can, even if that means selling some things

- If you must miss payments, do so carefully so you can recover quickly when things turn around.

- If things do not turn around quickly, protect the assets you can.

- Get professional legal and financial help if you cannot make ends meet.

CHAPTER THIRTEEN

After you have the job...

Content makes poor men rich; discontent makes rich men poor.

Benjamin Franklin

Once you have secured an adequate job, take a deep breath. You have succeeded! You have attained your goal! You are re-employed, perhaps even in your dream job.

Relaxing into a new position or career might be easier said than done. If your journey to re-employment took more than a few months, your career search may be engrained in almost everything you do. Perhaps you developed a routine of searching job listing websites or other resources on a daily basis. But, now you need to make that a part of your past, not your present.

Give it your all

Now that you are re-employed, your primary energy and effort should be directed to doing your best at your new job. For the time being, stop looking for something better and instead focus on being the best employee you can be. Your new employer will notice your commitment level and if she perceives you are less than fully committed, you may have to begin another job search.

Settling in to your new position will require time. Adjusting to new coworkers, policies, procedures, and company culture may take several months. You may become discouraged soon after starting a new job, but that may just be a normal stress reaction to the change you experience from starting a new position, perhaps even a new career.

Devoting your full efforts to your new job does not mean you will be perfect right from the start. You will make mistakes. You will not know everything you think you should know for this position. You may even feel incompetent at times. This, just like everything you experienced during your unemployed is quite normal. Making mistakes and feeling inadequate are all part of the adjustment process.

When you do not know something, do not be afraid to ask questions. It is much better to ask questions and risk appearing incompetent than to act in ignorance and become incompetent. There is a huge difference between being ignorant and teachable. Asking appropriate questions displays your willingness to your supervisor and coworkers that you want to ensure you perform your job correctly.

Just as you are adjusting to your new position, your supervisor and coworkers are adjusting to you. They are evaluating your willingness to take on extra duties and responsibilities as well as your willingness to learn. Giving your new job your full attention will keep you in tune to the expectations of those around you. Do your best to meeting or exceeding those expectations.

Delete your résumé

Many job listing websites allow you to post your résumé for potential employers to view. If you have uploaded your résumé to any of these, remove it as soon as you start your new position. You do not want your new boss to inadvertently find your résumé posted online. Even though you posted it months earlier, your supervisor does not know that. She may think you are not happy and are already looking for a position. Do not let an old résumé cost you a new job.

Post-employment depression

After successfully achieving a significant goal, some people enter a period of depression. This may happen to you after you have finally journeyed all the way from unemployment to re-employment. This may seem difficult for you to understand these feelings because you should be happy after seeing the fruits of your efforts. Just like entering a period of depression during unemployment is normal, so are melancholy feelings after you become re-employed.

Expending significant mental, physical and emotional energy toward achieving goals such as completing a degree or training program, and then becoming employed is taxing. After achieving the goals you worked so hard to attain, you may actually lose some of your sense of purpose. These feelings may be stronger if you are naturally a goal oriented person. Consider making a new goal of being the best you can be at your new job or career.

You may also have given yourself unrealistic expectations about the new job or career. You may even be wondering if you made a mistake choosing this job or career. These feelings too are normal. It takes time to adjust to new people, a new job, or a new career. Give yourself at least six months in the new position before you evaluate your choice. In the meantime, relax and enjoy the success of your hard work.

Open your eyes, look within. Are you satisfied with the life you're living?

Bob Marley

DOWN BUT NOT OUT

Key Points/Action Steps

- After you have a job, get out of search mode

- Put all your efforts into your new position

- Delete résumés you have posted online

- Some melancholy is normal after achieving the goal of becoming re-employed.

Part II:
It's my story and I'm sticking to it

DOWN BUT NOT OUT

Experience, the master educator, succeeds in making fools of us all.

Luther Maddy

Like the guy on the television commercials selling hairpieces, I am not only the author of this book, I am also a client. This book is partially the result of my education and professional experience. But, the most important sources of this book were my own mid-life career and subsequent financial crises. In short, I have not only studied the effects of lengthy unemployment, I have lived them firsthand. To help you better understand the lens through which I wrote this book, here is a glimpse into my own life.

CHAPTER FOURTEEN
Voluntary and involuntary changes

By three methods we may learn wisdom: First, by reflection, which is noblest; second, by imitation, which is easiest; and third by experience, which is the bitterest.

Confucius

In 1997, I resigned from a fairly secure job with a state government agency. After seven years of providing computer application training to this department's employees and receiving a steady paycheck with great benefits, I decided to risk everything and start my own business. Soon after leaving this job, my largest client was my former employer. I was also providing computer training to other government and private industry clients. The paychecks were larger, but certainly not as regular.

My decision to start and manage a small business was not as irrational as it may seem at first. Before starting this venture, I performed enough research to know I would be able to attract a substantial number of training engagements from my former employer. In addition, before working for this state agency, I had owned and operated my own computer sales and service business for several years.

Self-employment was not new to me. For better or for worse, I have been my own boss for most of my working life. Until recently reaching the age of 54, other than four years in the military, I was someone else's full-time employee for only eight of the thirty two years I had been in the workforce. There are certainly benefits to being self-employed, but there are disadvantages too. I was never as successful as I had hoped I would be, but those details are coming.

Reaping the rewards of entrepreneurship

My life was fairly good as a small businessman. By contracting with my former employer I was able to become profitable almost immediately. There were the normal ups and downs in my business, but we weathered them fairly well. Before too long I had transitioned my computer training business into a vocational school that provided training for people who became unemployed and wanted to change careers. We trained them quickly and allowed many to reenter the workforce and begin earning wages again.

I earned an adequate living, spending most all of it and sometimes spending more than I made. With the little I had left, I decided to follow the advice of that incredible financial expert Mark Twain who admonished me to buy real estate because they were not making it any more. I invested my profits in real estate. I purchased rental properties and moved several times, into a larger home each time. My mortgage payments increased with each new home's square footage.

I should have probably researched my primary financial advisor a little more before following his sage advice. Had I done so, I would have discovered that Samuel Clemens had his own financial crisis in his later years and eventually filed for bankruptcy protection. To his credit, he did pay all the discharged debts after recovering financially though he was not legally obligated to do so.

Within a few years of starting my business, I was living in a very nice home on three acres and managing five of my own

VOLUNTARY AND INVOLUNTARY CAREER CHANGES

rental properties. I cashed out my retirement plan from my years as a state employee for the down payment on that home. This did not worry me in the least because at the rate real estate was appreciating, I was sure real estate was the only retirement plan I would ever need.

Life was good. I was living the dream. I was in the maintenance stage of my career and looking forward to even better times. While my business had ups and downs, I was certain I would eventually be able to retire on my real estate holdings alone.

Life as I knew it ceased to exist

My life changed drastically in early 2005. The changes began with a phone call from my wife's family. My wife's brother had ended his life after a lengthy battle with depression.

Losing a loved one is never easy, but when it happens this way it elicits a tremendous amount of guilt. The "if only's" appeared often and without warning for several months. My wife's grief and soul searching resulted in her drawing very close to her family. Losing her brother affected her profoundly.

Less than four months after this tragedy, my wife's sister was diagnosed with leukemia. Her prognosis was a little better than 50/50. But, since their mother had won a battle against this same cancer a few years earlier, we assumed the same would be true for her. We assumed she would be fine after a few treatments. We hoped and prayed for the best but questioned why this was happening now.

Four months after her sister's diagnosis, my wife was diagnosed with a rare, technically incurable, form of lymphoma. She opted to undergo chemotherapy treatments anyway, hoping this would give her a few more years to spend with me and our two children. Perhaps, we reasoned, she would even be among the two percent of patients who lived beyond five years after this diagnosis. It was certainly worth the chance and the expense.

During this time I was essentially numb to the world and my business. I put in some time at work, but my real job was to care for and encourage my wife. I also saw myself as needing to be strong and prepare her, myself, and our two children for the inevitable outcome of her illness.

Her doctor prescribed a treatment method that was still somewhat experimental but had shown promising results in many patients. She was to undergo a total of five rounds of very extensive chemotherapy that required hospital stays. The doctor encouraged us both by speaking in terms of three to five years in the future.

My wife endured three rounds of chemotherapy. Every one ended up with her staying longer in the hospital than planned. If something could go wrong, it usually did. Her doctor stopped the treatments after three of the scheduled five rounds saying anymore chemotherapy would kill her.

The inevitable came much sooner than we planned. Ten months and several additional rounds of chemotherapy later, my wife lost her battle with lymphoma. Seven months after my wife's passing, her sister also lost her battle to leukemia. Three of my mother-in-law's four children were gone in a period of just over two years.

Those two years took an incredible toll on my emotions and my finances. In addition to the emotional scars I incurred during this time, I also incurred something else: debt. During my wife's illness I did not give my business my full attention. Revenues dropped substantially during her illness when I saw caring for her as my primary job.

I also incurred additional expenses after my wife was no longer able to work with me in my business. I had to hire an additional employee to handle her duties. Revenues were lower and expenses were higher. The seeds of a financial storm had been sown, though the full impact of this storm was still a couple of years away.

In the midst of tragedy and grief, our decision making processes do not always function at their best. Faced with lower revenues, higher expenses and decreased decision making

VOLUNTARY AND INVOLUNTARY CAREER CHANGES

capacity, I borrowed to keep the business afloat and to ensure my personal obligations, including a few medical bills, were met. We had very good medical insurance at the time, but even then, some treatment costs remained for me to pay. I even had to borrow money to pay for her funeral expenses. I had no liquid assets, all my net worth was tied up in real estate.

Being overly optimistic while my wife was being treated, I reasoned I could easily turn things around once I was able to give my business my full attention, after my wife was in remission. I also began divesting myself of some of my rentals to assist in making my substantial house and other loan payments.

While I would like to blame my circumstances for all of my financial mismanagement, I cannot. Even before my world was turned upside down, I had always lived very close to the tipping point. My financial carelessness was about to catch up with me.

CHAPTER FIFTEEN

A new start and risky behavior

When you play it too safe, you're taking the biggest risk of your life. Time is the only wealth we're given.
Barbara Sher

After my wife's passing, time slowed to a standstill. The hours seemed like days and the days, weeks. I had an overwhelming since of loneliness and loss. I continued to work at my school daily because it was somewhere I could be. Somewhere I had to be. Somewhere I was needed. However, I was there in body, but certainly not in spirit or mind. But still, it gave me something to do and kept me somewhat occupied.

After what seemed nearly an eternity, I remarried. I married a lady I had met in person only six weeks before we exchanged our wedding vows. This was just a little over seven months after my wife's passing, but at the time it seemed several lifetimes had passed. My new wife was also widowed, having lost her spouse one year earlier than I lost mine.

My new wife and I both loved our children, grandchildren, and each other dearly. However, we had a heightened sense of how short life can actually be. This translated into uncharacteristically risky behavior for both of us. For example, I bought a motorcycle and put my new wife on the back. When we rode, we rode fast, dodging in and out of traffic. We wore helmets when they were required by law. We did not have a death wish, but we both set out to enjoy life to the fullest, something neither of us had done much in the last couple of years. And, if our number was called in the process, so be it.

My new "don't care all that much" attitude also carried over into my business. Revenues had increased again and it was once again providing me with a nice income. My failure to avoid risk resulted in my decision to expand my vocational school into multiple locations. My first satellite location opened just after the first anniversary of my wife's passing. My son managed this location and it reached profitability quickly.

In less than two years after opening my first satellite location, I had a total of eight locations. All but two were making money. I had grown my business from a staff of two to twenty-one. And, I had done this without increasing my debt load at all. However, throwing good financial sense out the window with my new attitude, I spent all my profits on expansion, leaving nothing in reserve. I reasoned this would be no problem because all but two locations were already profitable. When one of my long term employees inquired about our financial stability, I answered, "I'm either going to be very rich, or go bankrupt trying." I could not have known how prophetic that statement actually was.

My house of cards collapses

Less than six months after opening my eighth location, I shut it down. This was my first foray into another state and a change in that state's rules shortly after we opened caused this location to languish with almost no revenue whatsoever. This mistake was expensive, but as long as my revenues continued at their existing level, I reasoned I could easily absorb the loss.

One month after closing my newest satellite location, I had no inkling that things were about to change. But my financial condition did change and it changed rapidly. Over the next twelve months my revenues dropped every month. That year ended with

A NEW START AND RISKY BEHAVIOR

revenues not quite one-half the previous year's figures. My expenses, however, did not drop substantially, even after closing the unprofitable location.

Instead of improving, things got worse. I began closing other locations as they began losing money in an effort to stop the huge losses I was incurring each month. One year after closing my eighth location, I was down to four locations. Three months later I had contracted to only two locations.

In another effort to further cut expenses, I stopped paying myself early in the year of our contraction. To make my house payment and other expenses, I began selling what I could. I sold coins, firearms I had owned for years, and collectibles I had recently acquired. I became very familiar with online auctions and classified websites. A few months later my credit cards were maxed out and I had sold almost everything I had of value. It was then that I finally faced the realization that I was going to have to miss payments for the first time in my life.

While things were going well, I also made my new wife an employee of the business, but her paychecks stopped as well. Without those paychecks, her part-time job at a local hospital did not provide enough income to meet the expenses she came to the marriage with, let alone assist with my massive debt load.

Time to get a job

While I certainly respect the captain of the Titanic's decision to not leave his sinking ship, I did not share his sentiments. I could see the writing on the wall and I was certain I was on a sinking ship. I did not want to get sucked into the huge whirlpool my collapsing business was causing. In an attempt to save my few remaining personal assets and credit rating, I began applying for jobs, any job.

I sat down and dug out my old résumé. I then applied for my first full-time job since starting my business some 13 years earlier. That first application started the process that eventually resulted in the writing of this book. The progression of transforming from small business owner to full-time employee would take more than three years. It was a journey that would take me through twenty-one interviews, foreclosures, and bankruptcy before it ended.

As I stated previously, I am not only the author of this book, I am also a client. I have lived with the rejection of not being hired. I have made the tough decisions of what to pay and what not to pay. I have even lived with not being able to pay any of my obligations. I have also watched helplessly as my real estate holdings, my only retirement plan, decreased in value and quickly became liabilities.

But, my story does not end in defeat and neither should your story end where you are today. My story is one of overcoming rejection, a story of dusting myself off and starting over with almost nothing. Sharing my story will hopefully show you that things will get better. Yes, it will take work, courage, faith, and support, but you too can learn not to be defined by your current circumstances. There is life beyond unemployment and here is some more of my story to illustrate that fact.

Pursing Additional Education

A year or two into my new marriage we began transitioning back into our more conservative selves. My wife, looking toward the future, began to encourage me to further my education. She also began to encourage me to consider what my life could be like outside of my small business. Fortunately, she did this before thinking about this became a necessity.

I had completed a master's degree nearly twenty years earlier and that was enough education for me, or so I thought. My wife was continuing her own education and it seemed like a considerable amount of work and effort. But, primarily to appease my new wife, I enrolled in classes at a local university.

Imagine my surprise when I discovered I enjoyed being back in school. Within the first few weeks, these classes re-ignited my love for learning. When I first enrolled I had no intentions of pursuing a new degree, taking a few classes was a great way to spend some time. As the semester continued I found the classes were very relevant to my current business and provided very useful information to help me better manage my then booming business and its many instructors.

My reluctance to pursue a new degree was short-lived. Several weeks into my first semester, I applied for and was eventually accepted into a Ph.D. program. Convincing the members of the acceptance interview committee to allow me into the program was not difficult. After all, I was a successful small businessman ready to upgrade my education. A Ph.D. would be just another feather in my cap. I possessed more than enough arrogance then, but it was very short lived.

It was near the end of the next semester, shortly after I was accepted into the degree program that I began to apply for jobs out of financial necessity. Although I was just two semesters into the program, I emphasized my new educational pursuits on my résumé and cover letter. I was still a few years away from completing my degree, but I was sure being accepted to the program would make me a much more viable candidate for any job, at least that is what I thought.

Waning Optimism

I was 51 years of age when I decided to flee my failing business and give up a life of self-employment. I was certain finding a new job would be a relatively quick and easy task. After all, my business had been helping people transition into new careers for several years. Surely, my business expertise, education, and irresistible charm would enable me to quickly maneuver into a high paying corporate training management position. I expected to be employed and earning a sizeable paycheck in no time. Once employed, I would be able to make all my payments and could stop looking around the house for things to sell on online auction sites.

Reality set in very soon. As I scoured the newspaper and online job boards, I saw very few openings in my field of expertise in the local area. Granted, part of the problem was that I did not really have a field of expertise. My background was quite diverse.

DOWN BUT NOT OUT

I had experience in information technology, but my formal education was business related. I had concluded that my years of training adults in computer related topics, coupled with my successful years of owning a business would make me a hot commodity. I was very wrong.

Desperate to save my home and credit rating before they were irreparably damaged, I mailed and uploaded dozens of résumés and cover letters. I scrutinized the popular job listing websites for openings across the nation. I applied for any job that was even closely related to my qualifications and experience. The location of the job did not matter anymore. I desperately needed income because I was running out of things to sell.

After applying for several dozen jobs, I sat by the phone and waited, but the phone calls did not come. I developed an obsession for checking my email every few minutes, but there were no job offers in my inbox either.

CHAPTER SIXTEEN

Interview Hell

Pessimism of the spirit; optimism of the will.
                                    Antonio Gramsci

    I could hardly contain my excitement when I got the phone call for my first interview. I had applied for the position of training manager at a large local company. I was sure this position was the answer to my prayers. It was local and paid well. It was certainly meant to be. I had not yet missed my first payment on any obligations and was sure I could squeak by until I started this new job.

    The day of the interview I was understandably nervous. There was much at stake and this was my first interview in many years. I showed up in my best attire, and despite my nerves, I was sure I would impress them and probably get a job offer on the spot. I cannot say I suffered from lowered levels of self-esteem at this point. I still had much to learn, I just did not know it at the time.

    I prepared as well as I could for this interview. I studied the textbooks from the classes I was taking. I filled my head with the jargon and theories I was sure would impress those interviewing me. I envisioned the interview many times in my head beforehand. In my mind, the scenario always ended with me getting a job offer. I had not even considered the alternative.

Unfortunately, the interview did follow the script I had laid out in my head. It did not go nearly well as I had envisioned. After the usual questions about my background and experience, the three member interview panel started asking some very difficult questions. Unfortunately, I found I was not prepared for the questions they asked.

They asked me several questions about things I had never heard of, even after taking several classes in my current pursuit of a degree in adult education and organizational leadership. I convinced myself they were just behind the times. I was learning all the latest theories and those were not what they were inquiring about. Granted, I had never actually applied most of the theories I was reading about. But still, I anticipated my newfound knowledge would counter my lack of actual corporate training management experience.

When my inquisitors asked me questions I could not answer, I told them that I would surely be learning about that topic in an upcoming class. I also informed them I was a very fast learner and would certainly know the answers by the time I started my new job. These responses did not appear to satisfy the panel.

As the interview ended, I was fairly sure my delay tactics to the tough questions were not sufficient for this firm. They told me they would be making the hiring decision later that week. I hoped I would receive another phone call, but knew deep inside that it was not very likely. I did not hold my breath and eventually received a "thanks for coming in" letter.

My still fairly new wife was very helpful at this time. She was very understanding and offered much needed encouragement. She also helped me focus on one career for my new job search. Her statement was essentially, "We're in a real mess and it doesn't look like there is any quick way out. So, you may as well aim for the job you really want".

INTERVIEW HELL

With my wife's encouragement, and it truly was encouraging, I began pursuing a job I had dreamed of for years, being a college professor. I had the right degrees and was in the midst of earning another. I also had years of experience teaching, although no actual experience teaching college classes. I also really missed being in the classroom. I had not been able to teach since expanding my business and focusing on its management and most recently, focusing on its survival.

So, rather than continuing to send out hundreds of résumés for corporate training jobs, I switched gears. I then sent out hundreds of résumés to colleges and universities. It did not matter to me where the school was located. As long as I met the minimum qualifications, or was close, I applied. The result was essentially the same. I waited by the phone and my computer to no avail.

A few nerve wracking weeks went by and then I received a phone call from a college in Southern Texas. This was a long way from Idaho, but it was a job. After a phone interview that I was sure I had bombed, I received an invitation to interview in person. The college was happy to reimburse me for my travel and lodging after the interview. I borrowed money for a plane ticket from family and flew to Texas.

The position in Texas involved both teaching and managing. It seemed perfect, but it was far from either of our families. Unlike my last attempt, this interview seemed to go very well. In addition to the usual interview questions, it also involved a teaching demonstration, which I had plenty of time to prepare for. I left this interview feeling much better than when I left the interview for the corporate training manager several weeks earlier. Perhaps teaching college is where I indeed belonged.

After returning to Idaho, I quickly asked for feedback from a member of the interview panel via email. I was told I had done very well at the interview. This bolstered my hopes and I began moving to Texas, at least mentally.

DOWN BUT NOT OUT

Two long weeks later I received an email from the college in Texas. The email informed me that the position was pulled due to budget constraints and would not be filled at this time. It would be re-opened if and when their finances changed. There was no estimate of when the position might be reopened.

Two interviews down and no job offer. That month I missed by first credit card payment. I sold some more household items and my son's car to make my house payment. I did not know it at the time, but that would be the last house payment I would make on that home.

A few weeks after hearing from Texas, I received another invitation to interview at a college about seven hours away in the state of Washington. I was not reimbursed for my travel expenses for this interview. I have since learned this is a very big red flag. But, blissfully ignorant at the time, I headed off to Washington hoping and praying that I could stave off financial ruin and become employed quickly.

The interview went well, or so I thought. After checking back a few days later I was told I was in the background checking phase. While I had not received an offer or any commitment whatsoever, I was sure this was the job for me, just like the last two. This time, I began moving more than mentally. I packed up my office, sold a few of my wife's possessions that I did not want to move and waited for the offer.

An offer did not come. The position went to a part-time instructor they already knew. I requested some feedback on the interview process and was told I interviewed very well. I had heard that before. I was also told that one significant weak spot on my résumé was a lack of recent college teaching experience. Most of my recent experience was managing, not teaching and I had still never taught a class that issued college credits.

Due to a temporary lapse of judgment, heightened by my latest rejection and humiliation of packing to move before I received an offer, I applied for a position as a research analyst. I did not actually know what a research analyst did, but I met the

INTERVIEW HELL

minimum requirements, so I applied. This firm was local and was growing rapidly. I did enough research on this firm to know it was a young company, staffed with many young employees.

Surprisingly, I received an invitation to interview with this firm for the position of research analyst shortly after submitting my résumé. Knowing a little about this company's culture, I decided I needed to do my best to look younger. I shaved my graying beard the day before the interview. I walked into the interview room that day with a clean shaven face. But, I also had a definite tan-line revealing where my beard had been the day before.

This interview went very well, for the first five minutes. Then the grilling began. It quickly morphed from interview to examination. For nearly two hours I was bombarded with questions that tested my statistical knowledge, my critical thinking abilities, and my knowledge of computer programming languages.

This interview was like a tag team wrestling match. When one team tired of hitting me with brain teasers, a fresh team of inquisitors would take their place. I left that two-hour interview exhausted, mentally and physically. I also left knowing I would not be working as a research analyst. I did, however, leave having an idea of what research analysts did. But, since I did not care about the chances of picking a red piece of candy from a bowl filled with mostly blue ones, I knew a career as a research analyst was not for me. I also quit shaving again. Gray or not, my beard was coming back.

The torture session at the analytics firm got me back on track. I was now completely sure I wanted to teach college. I was also sure I never ever wanted anything to do with statistics.

In the next few months I interviewed in person at two colleges in California and one in Minnesota. Neither of the schools in California offered to pay my travel expenses. They simply invited me to interview and expected me to pay my own way, which I did. I still had not learned.

The college in Minnesota did reimburse me for travel expenses. I interviewed for a fairly high-level position in administration. This position was a stretch, but I applied anyway. I was actually very surprised to receive an invitation to interview for this administrative position. I knew within the first minute of the interview, it was a waste of time for me and every one of the thirty people on the interview panel. My rejection letter informed me they had hired someone "more qualified" for the position. That was not hard for them to do.

I also had a few telephone interviews. My applications resulted in phone interviews with a few more colleges in Colorado and Texas. That is as far as I got with those schools. I heard nothing at all from dozens of other colleges across the country.

I started my job hunt self-confident and a little arrogant. But, the rejections were beginning to take their toll. My self-esteem, my overall feelings of self-worth, began to suffer. I was beginning to consider myself a complete failure in life. I was a failure at business and a failure at finding a job.

Perhaps worse than the feeling of failure was the uncertainty of what the future held. I did not know where I would be living or how I would be earning an income. I was, however, fairly certain I would be moving very soon since I was no longer making my mortgage payments.

Filing for unemployment

Desperate for income of any kind, I laid myself off from the business I started. I had not been working there much recently anyway and I had not been paid for several months. I had three employees remaining at that time and informed them to save the business if they could, but I was stepping away.

After stepping away from managing my business I filed for unemployment. I received just over $1,200 per month. This amount did not even come close to helping me meet my enormous financial obligations. Instead, I used this money to fund two of my trips to interview out of state. I still did not understand what the organization's unwillingness to pay travel expenses

INTERVIEW HELL

usually meant. I wasted much of my unemployment compensation traveling to interview for jobs that I had no chance of getting.

My unemployment income also assured that I could continue to eat, which is something I have always greatly enjoyed. It also assured I could assist with the household expenses including utilities, life insurance, and other important expenses. Since neither my late wife nor my current wife's late husband had life insurance when they passed away, making our life insurance payments was a very high priority. After nearly a year with no income at all, even the small amount I was receiving from unemployment was very reassuring.

CHAPTER SEVENTEEN

Transitioning into a new career

Success is not final, failure is not fatal: it is the courage to continue that counts.
                                               Winston Churchill

    Perhaps it was having even a tiny amount of money coming in, or maybe it was giving up on my business altogether, but whatever the reason, I began to think a little clearer. I recalled a common theme from some of the feedback I was receiving from the colleges I interviewed with. The shortcoming on my résumé I heard several times was that I lacked actual experience teaching at the college level. For some reason, instructing at the corporate or vocational school level was not the same in their eyes. I needed to add college instruction to my résumé if I was ever going to get a job as a college professor. I decided I could do that by teaching part-time, being an adjunct instructor, for any of the many colleges and universities in my local area.

    While I began to think a little clearer, by this time, my self-image was at an all-time low. I leaned heavily on my wife for support during this time. The encouragement she and other family members provided helped counter the negative pressure my self-esteem was receiving from external circumstances. Those close to me became an essential support system and they kept reminding me that I was not worthless, but had much to offer. They also helped me focus on successes in the past and continually encouraged me not to let myself be defined by these temporary circumstances.

My personal faith also played a significant role in my support during this time. Being a Christian, I knew I was loved by God and that He chose to adopt me into His family. That belief gave me a strong foundation of self-worth, even though the turmoil and emotions of the moment exerted very strong negative influences.

I also called out to God continually in prayer. I pleaded for guidance and rescue. When neither came as quickly as I expected, I did not understand. I did, however, have confidence that "...God causes everything to work together for the good of those who love God and are called according to his purpose for them.[13]"

I believed those words, but still wondered about what the immediate future held in store. My experiences from just a few years earlier helped me realize that God does not always let us write our own stories. Sometimes we journey on a road that is not of our choosing. However, the foundations of my faith helped me look past my current circumstances toward my journey's destination, re-employment in my dream job.

While my faith and family support should have kept me continually optimistic, it did not work that way. I often let myself wallow in the mire of depression and self-pity. Faith and family support helped pull me out whenever I neared the point of no return.

Even in the midst of these trials, my pride and arrogance popped up now and then, but a quick reality check usually got them below the surface. I also realized the feelings of self-sufficiency I harbored for years were not helping in this situation. As a result, I did something I would have never done in my

---

[13] Romans 8:28, New Living Translation. 2007

previous arrogance and feeling of self-sufficiency, I asked for help from a family friend who was a professor at a local university.

I reached out to this family friend with an email. I asked her to review my résumé. I also asked if I could use her as a reference during my job hunt. I also shared that I was having difficulty getting hired. I did not share my financial distress or why finding a job was so urgent. Though I did not share this information, being a friend of the family, she likely already knew.

Reaching out to this family friend for help proved incredibly worthwhile. Not only did she provide some excellent suggestions for improving my résumé, she also suggested that I send it to the head of the business department at the university where she was employed. She mentioned she would put in a good word for me.

Thanks to assistance of this family friend, two weeks later I found myself interviewing for a part-time teaching position with this university. Unlike the so many before, this interview was successful. I was offered a part-time teaching position and would be teaching courses the very next semester.

The semester start was still a couple of months away, but I would be earning nearly $1,000 a month for five months. This was not as much as I was making on unemployment, but it was enough to give me the boost I needed. I was finally going to be a college professor, if only part-time. And, if I proved my skills in the classroom, I could expect additional teaching assignments from this university.

In January of that year, the week before classes started, I stopped my unemployment checks. I had received them for three months, but now I was employed, even if only part-time. When I started teaching these classes, I laid off another one of my employees and returned to my business. I did not receive a paycheck for this and reducing the expenses of my business by one more employee helped it begin to stabilize.

Learning financial lessons the hard way

When I began teaching part-time, I was no longer making any payments on my debt obligations. I had stopped all of those several months earlier. Seeing no other way out, I filed for Chapter 7 bankruptcy a few weeks before my part-time paychecks started arriving. I left this process no longer owning my rental properties and knowing I must soon leave my home because foreclosure was imminent.

Bankruptcy laws allow for certain amounts and types of property to be exempt from seizure in those proceedings. The most common exempt properties include equity in a home and retirement accounts. I had neither. I did leave still owning my motorcycle and some of our furniture. I had earlier tried to sell my motorcycle at a great price to make a house payment, but no one took me up on the offer.

The motorcycle my wife paid for with her own funds was considered non-exempt property. It was due to be auctioned off to pay my numerous creditors. Fortunately, I was able to work out a payment plan with my trustee and buy it back. It took several months for me to do this, but I may have saved my new marriage in the process.

My wife took another route with her debts. Rather than filing for bankruptcy she began working with a credit counseling firm. The multiyear arrangement she worked out with them allowed her to pay off all her obligations at reduced interest rates.

Before choosing the bankruptcy route myself, I contacted several debt counseling firms. Unfortunately, they all told me the same thing. I needed some income to pay my bills. With no income, they could not help me. They simply did not understand that if I did have income, I would not have contacted them and I would not have been behind on my bills.

Filing bankruptcy is not something I admit with pride. It is the ultimate admission of failure and bad judgment. The last few years of my life had been marked with severe loss, financial crisis, turmoil, and uncertainty. Bankruptcy provided a sense of closure for much of my chaos and allowed me to move forward. The decision to file for bankruptcy was probably largely responsible for me keeping my sanity through this entire process.

TRANSITIONING INTO A NEW CAREER

When my first paycheck arrived from the university that hired me, I purchased at 14 year old car for less than $2,000. I had sold my favorite vehicle several months earlier to make mortgage payments. I voluntarily surrendered another vehicle that I had stopped making payments on the same day I purchased my new old car. My new old car ran perfectly and got me to my new job as a part-time college professor.

The doors begin to open

I wasted no time placing my newly acquired "real" college teaching experience on my résumé. I had previously applied numerous times for part-time teaching positions at all the colleges in my area to no avail. It seemed no one wanted to be the first to take a chance on me. I had considerable teaching experience on my résumé, but nothing in the college setting until that first semester.

Once the first university showed a willingness to trust me in their classrooms, other opportunities began to appear. Just before that semester ended I interviewed for a part-time teaching position and a local community college. The individual I interviewed with had recently graduated from the university where I was currently teaching. That was enough to get me to an interview this time, something I had never been able to do before. When this interview concluded, I was signed up to teach four classes that next fall.

Between the two colleges, I would be earning a livable wage. In all, I would be teaching five to six classes per semester. I would be teaching more classes than most full-time instructors teach, and would be doing it for less than one half the salary full-time instructors receive. Nevertheless, I was very happy to be earning money once again.

Knowing I would be earning income in the fall began to improve my damaged self-image, but the scars of so many previous rejections were still very visible. My self-efficacy was still very low. I had lost most of my confidence in my ability to teach. I was even fearful I would prove inadequate in the classroom and find myself unemployed again, even though I had more than twenty years of experience teaching.

By focusing on the fact that I was employed, and in the career I had aspired to, I was able to regain enough confidence to enter the classroom when the time came. As I did, I then set out to be the best college instructor I could be. Then, after proving my teaching ability, I could then just wait for a full-time position to open. Then, I thought, I could be the internal candidate that got hired instead of the outsider who came from out of state at his or her own expense.

Even while teaching a course load of six classes per semester, I was still a full-time student. Completing my degree was still almost two years away. But, I was earning money and I actually enjoyed the stress of preparing for and teaching so many classes each semester at different locations. Staying so busy kept my mind off losing my house, rentals, cars, and almost everything else. And, working part-time for these two colleges was certainly better than the alternative.

Network, network, network!

People like to hire people they know, or people recommended by someone they know and trust. I learned this the hard way, which is actually how I learn most things. My feelings of self-sufficiency caused me to isolate myself to the world of my own small business. It was not until I reached out for help and networked, that I achieved any success at all in my efforts to change careers.

The concept of people hiring people they know was responsible for me getting another, career changing, teaching opportunity. Before being hired to teach for the first university, I visited with a department head at the largest university in my local area. During this cordial visit I casually inquired about potential adjunct teaching opportunities, but I was there primarily to solicit advice about the Ph.D. I was pursuing. I wanted to ensure it would qualify me to teach full-time at a university such as this one. I also asked several questions about my upcoming dissertation.

Receiving assurance that my degree would suffice, I thanked the department chair for his time and dissertation advice. I followed up this visit with a résumé, but heard nothing in response.

After waiting more than a year after my first visit with the department chair at this university, I sent another résumé. Unlike my first one, this résumé showed actual experience in a college classroom with two other colleges in the area. Other schools had already taken the chance on me. I was no longer an unknown quantity.

In the educational community, timing is very important. I was learning that hiring decisions for the next semester were made early in the prior semester. I sent my résumé to the department chair at this university a month after the spring semester began. I was hoping there might be an opening in the fall. I had already learned that teaching positions were not something you started immediately.

This time, however, it was a little different. Four days after sending my résumé via email, I found myself in a meeting with the department head again. This time it was a job interview. He informed me that an instructor was retiring mid-semester, which left an immediate opening.

Because of our previous meeting, this interview was extremely comfortable. He already knew me. He already knew I was open to his advice. And, because of my newly enhanced résumé, he also knew I could handle myself in the classroom.

Less than one month after this interview, I was in the classroom at this large university. This turned out to be a team teaching opportunity. I shared instructional duties with another part-time instructor who had been affiliated with this university for many years. Being my own boss for so many years caused me to approach team teaching with a little apprehension, but in the end, this also became another excellent networking opportunity. I also made a friend in the process.

I was not happy with my performance in that class that semester. Taking over for another instructor mid-semester is not an easy task, especially when our approach was completely different. I was sure our student evaluations would not be good and I was almost certain I would never teach for this university again after that semester ended.

My assumptions, as usual, were wrong. Shortly after that semester ended I received a phone call from Cheryl Larabee. She invited me to interview for another part-time teaching position at this university. I had not previously met Cheryl but researched her a little before after the phone call. My research helped me understand the importance of this interview and the possibility of being able to work with her.

Later that week, I found myself sitting down at an interview with Cheryl. Yes, I was interviewing for another part-time team teaching opportunity, but this one was different. It was to be the launch of an entirely new class at this university. It would be two classes of 180 students each, something I had not previously even imagined.

Cheryl and I had never previously met. I had not even ever sent her a résumé. I was there because I had been recommended for this position by the department chair and the instructor I had teamed up with that previous semester.

Networking had paid off again. When that next fall arrived, I was teaching for three colleges. Most of my time however, went to the new course offering at the large university. It was much more like a full-time job, but with very little pay. However, the knowledge I gained and the people I became acquainted with during this time made it very worthwhile. In the midst of this course rollout, I jokingly remarked that I should be paying for the experience rather than begin paid.

The interview that counted

During my time as an adjunct instructor at three different institutions, I continued to apply for full-time positions all over the United States. For some reason, even though I now had more experience and education on my résumé, the calls to interview were not coming as quickly as they had before. I found this quite strange and my anxiety levels started to increase again.

I was due to finish my degree in the spring of that year. I was sure with the experience now on my résumé, as well as my terminal degree, I would be inundated with job offers. I also knew this year, after graduation would be my best chance of getting a full-time position.

Because I was still reeling from numerous rejections, I made the decision, after ensuring my wife was in agreement, to accept the first job I was offered at a location we both agreed was satisfactory. I did not want to turn down a steady paycheck for something that might be offered in the future. With that goal in mind, I narrowed my focus to colleges and universities within a day's drive of where we currently lived.

Shortly after making this decision, I received a phone call from the college in Texas I had interviewed with more than one year earlier. The position I had previously interviewed for reopened and I was invited to interview again. After considerable deliberation and prayer, I turned down the offer to interview. Texas was too far from either of our families.

Just a few days after turning down that interview, the university where I was earning my doctorate opened a position that seemed perfect for me. I applied. Once again I was sure this was the job for me. I was interviewed over the phone by one of my professors. Apparently, I did not have all the experience needed for this position. The search committee had misread my résumé. Or, at least that is what they said during the phone interview. That process ended with one more rejection to add to my growing list.

Just after that rejection, another school in the local area posted an opening for a position in my field. This was one of the few schools in the area I was not currently teaching for but, I was sure it was the job for me. It would be an easy transition. We would not need to move and the pay was adequate.

DOWN BUT NOT OUT

As I had done a few times previously, I began to envision working for this college. Mentally, I already had the job. I certainly had no problem with positive thinking. I was so sure I was going to get this job I set myself up for a huge letdown, again. I was invited to interview by telephone, but despite my best efforts, I did not make it past that level. This was my twentieth interview since beginning this process and I was now convinced my interviewing techniques needed to change dramatically.

After that disappointment I noticed an opening for a position at a college about 300 miles from where I was currently living. I submitted my résumé for their consideration. After doing this, I began to hear rumors at two of the colleges where I was currently teaching part-time. Both were expecting to add new full-time positions the next fall. However, nothing was official at this point.

Just a few weeks after the position 300 miles away closed, I received a phone call. My presence was requested at an interview. To add to my excitement, the institution volunteered to pay my travel expenses. The travel reimbursement let me know they were truly interested and I assumed, correctly or not, that this meant they had no local candidates in contention.

After so many failed interviews, I knew my interviewing skills needed improvement. It had been more than one year since I had interviewed in person for a full-time position. Not only was I a little rusty, I was feeling fairly insecure and not sure I could handle another rejection.

After evaluating my many failed interviews, I was beginning to understand the B.E.S.T. (Body Language, Enthusiasm, Smile, Think) technique explained earlier and was sure I would employ it for this interview. However, I needed some additional confidence before I could handle another interview. In fact, I was so afraid of another rejection I seriously considered withdrawing from consideration before the interview.

Because of my successful, albeit belated attempts at networking, I was working closely with Cheryl Larabee. Cheryl is a very accomplished businesswoman. Before coming to this university, she had many years in the banking industry. Prior to taking on the development of the new course offering, she was a vice president for development at this university and headed up fund raising efforts that resulted in several million dollars being donated to this institution. She has also served on several corporate boards including serving as a chairperson of the board for a publically traded electronic accessories firm. Cheryl was tasked with the major responsibilities of our huge classes of freshmen and I was fortunate enough to be team teaching with her.

Humbling myself a little, something I was finding much easier to do after struggling the last three years, I asked Cheryl for help. I explained that I believe my interviewing skills were somewhat lacking. I had forgotten that she had interviewed me herself and had hired me for this part-time position several months earlier.

Cheryl's gracious response to my inquiry was to share her R.I.C.H. method with me that you can find detailed in an earlier chapter. I found this incredibly easy to remember and employ. I ran though it several times before the day of the interview arrived.

Before the interview I also researched the college and some of the people I knew would be on the interview panel. I also learned that the interview process would include a five hour drive with the department chair to a satellite location and back. I spent more time learning what I could about the chair. This long drive meant I would have to spend a considerable amount of time in small talk and intelligent conversation. Using Cheryl's R.I.C.H. method, along with my B.E.S.T. technique proved to be perfect for this situation.

Too many decisions

The interview went very well. The teaching demonstration also went well. But, so had many of my other interviews, at least until I received the rejection letter or email. Still, something felt different about this interview process. While I waited for an answer either way, two of the colleges I was teaching at opened the rumored positions for applications. I submitted my applications and hoped I would receive an instant offer at one of these schools before being faced with the very difficult decision of packing up and moving 300 miles farther away from our families.

When the phone call that I had so desperately awaited finally came I was excited and apprehensive. It was just what I had expected so many times, but this time it actually happened. I was offered the position. I was being offered a full-time, tenure-track assistant professor position. The salary was higher than either of the positions I was waiting for locally. Still, picking up and moving at my age was not something I relished. But, since I no longer owned a home, the timing could not have been better.

Rather than immediately accepting the offer, I countered on a couple of minor issues. I gave them two days to respond. Since their counter offer was not everything I had asked for, I requested two additional days to make a decision. I was attempting to buy time. I had already decided to accept the first firm offer, but when an offer came I wavered and attempted to stall the decision. Perhaps this was a result of the utter turmoil I had experienced in the last few years. Or, perhaps it was simply fear.

I accepted their offer two hours before the deadline I had imposed on myself. I felt an immense sense of relief because I now knew I would be employed and where we would be living. Moving mentally all around the country with each interview had taken its toll. I was ready to settle in somewhere, anywhere.

Thirty minutes after I called and accepted the job offer, my phone rang. It was one of the local colleges wishing to interview me for one of their open positions. The pay was comparable to the position I had just accepted, but the job was not as appealing as the one I had just accepted.

As I turned down that interview, I felt an immense load of uncertainty being lifted from me. I had a job and it was my dream job at that. I was finally a full-time college professor. I had survived my career and financial crisis. I learned a considerable

TRANSITIONING INTO A NEW CAREER

amount in the process. I was, hopefully, a little wiser now. I was certainly older.

Though I ended my journey with essentially no financial assets, I had really learned some valuable lessons. Now I could finally begin the arduous task of rebuilding my career, credit, and finances. The only problem was that I would have to teach statistics.

Luther M. Maddy III holds a Ph.D in Adult and Organizational Learning and Leadership from the University of Idaho. He is currently an assistant professor in the Business Division at Lewis-Clark State College in Lewiston, Idaho where he lives with his wife Tracy. Luther also owns a vocational school he founded in 1997.

Luther is available to for speaking and training sessions elaborating on the information in Down But Not Out. For more information, visit Luther's website at: www.LutherMaddy.com

Full size forms from this book and other resources are available on Luther's website.

Also by Luther M. Maddy III
Available at all online retailers in print and e-book format.

Two Years on the Run

Two Years on the Run is the humorous story of Luther adjusting to a new marriage after losing his wife of nearly 28 years. Much of this story involves motorcycle trips through the Western and Midwestern United States. This book is available in print or as an e-book.

www.ingramcontent.com/pod-product-compliance
Lightning Source LLC
Chambersburg PA
CBHW051654170526
45167CB00001B/456